Woodcarving the Nativity

in the Folk Art Style

By Shawn Cipa

Fox Chapel Publishing
1970 Broad Street • East Petersburg, PA 17520
www.FoxChapelPublishing.com

Acknowledgments

Thanks to Fox Chapel for the opportunity to publish this book. Thanks to my father, Paul, who has taken valuable time to design this book for me. Last but not least, thanks to all the readers of my first book for their much appreciated words of praise. Keep carving!

Publisher Alan Giagnocavo
Book Editor Ayleen Stellhorn
Cover Design Jon Deck
Interior Photography Shawn Cipa
Desktop Specialist Paul Cipa

ISBN 1-56523-202-X
Library of Congress Preassigned Card Number: 2003107290

To order your copy of this book,
please send check or money order
for the cover price plus $3.50 shipping to:
Fox Chapel Publishing
Book Orders
1970 Broad St.
East Petersburg, PA 17520

Or visit us on the web at **www.FoxChapelPublishing.com**

Manufactured in China

10 9 8 7 6 5 4 3 2

Dedication

To Joe and Margaret
and the rest of my
family and friends,
and especially
to my wife, Joanne,
for her unending
support.

*And...
On that night
A King
was born.*

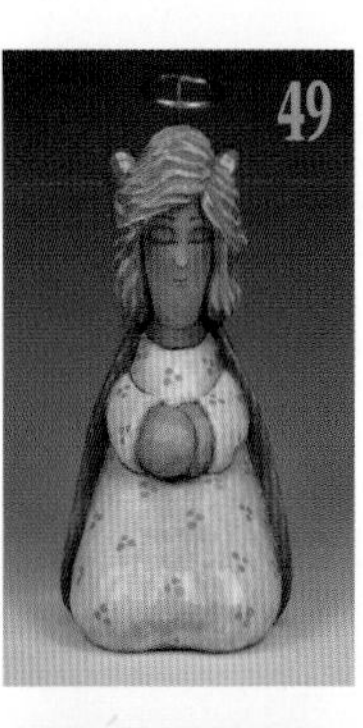

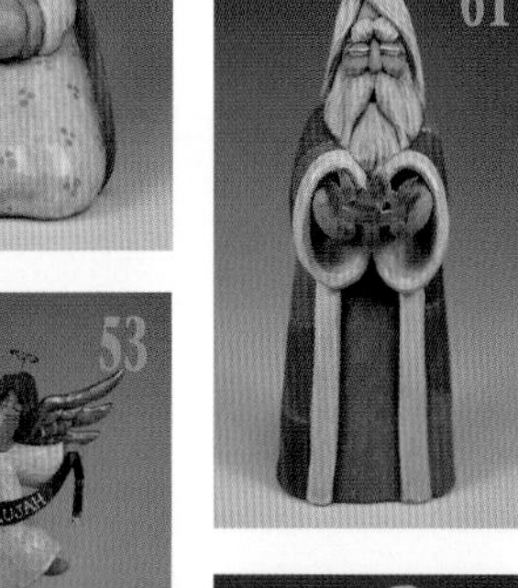

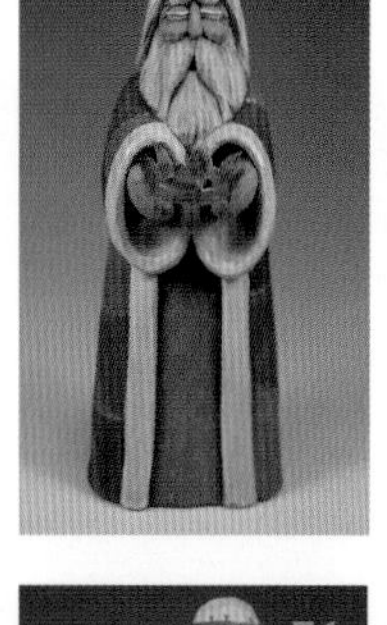

49 53 55 59 61 71 73 65 75 77 79 67

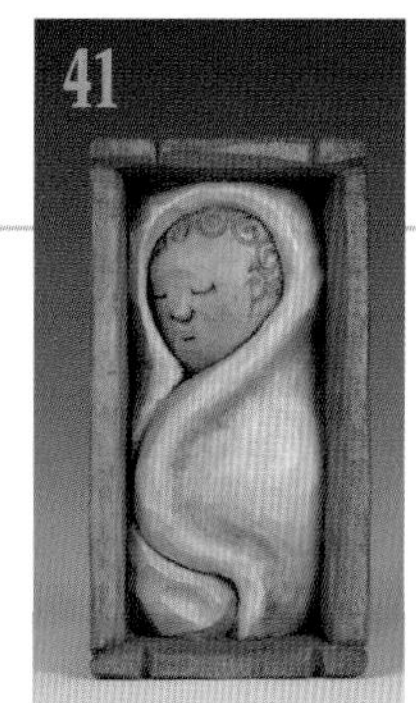

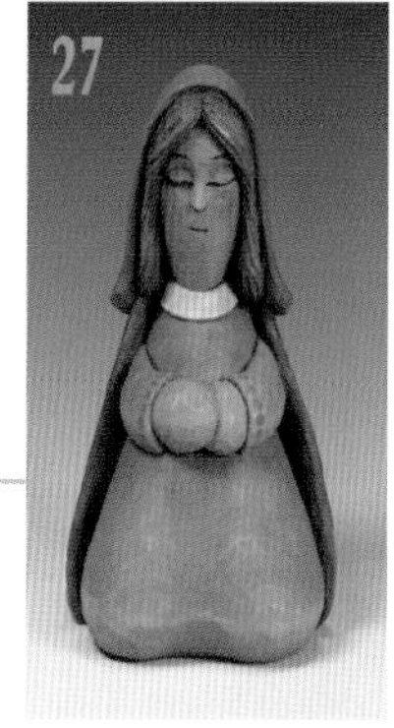

Table of Contents

About the Author

Shawn Cipa began carving in 1993 after his wife, Joanne, bought him a small set of palm tools for Christmas. Already possessing a solid background in art, Shawn found that woodcarving soon became a driving passion in his life. He began by carving wood spirits, and soon after tried his hand at Old Father Christmas. Although Shawn has carved many different subjects by commission, he admittedly prefers all things whimsical in nature. Walking sticks, canes, Santas, angels, and other mythical characters are just some of his repertoire.

Shawn comes from an artistic family and has experience in several art forms such as illustration, painting and sculpture. His mother, a free thinker, and his father, a successful graphic designer of several decades, provided the creative atmosphere necessary to spur him on and develop his skills. Although most art mediums came easy to Shawn, carving wasn't one of them. It was a daunting task to learn to sculpt by taking *away* rather than adding on as is done in clay sculpting. However, perseverance has paid off.

Shawn's other skills include carpentry, photography, and amateur astronomy. He is also an accomplished musician of many years, his passion for music rivaling his love of the visual arts.

Shawn was recognized as a national winner in Woodcraft Supply Corporation's 2000 Santa carving contest. He is also the author of *Carving Folk Art Figures*, available from Fox Chapel Publishing. Shawn does commission work from his website and provides pieces to many collectors internationally. He hopes to continue his carving endeavors with unending support from his wife, Joanne, as well as his family and friends who have helped to encourage him.

Please feel free to contact Shawn by visiting his Website at:
www.shawnscarvings.com

Introduction

When the opportunity of producing a Nativity carving project presented itself to me, I jumped at the idea. Long had I wanted to carve a nativity set but never seemed to have the time to work it all out. Now was my chance!

The story of the Nativity as a miraculous happening has been depicted in art form many times over and in many different ways. In the course of the last 2000 years, countless depictions have emerged from artists the world over, all striving to stir and uplift the soul of the observer. Sadly, in these modern times, the Nativity as an art object has often been cheapened. Low-grade reproductions made of resin and plastic combined with poor designs have reduced this symbol of faith into a cliché for many people. It is my hope that you will create something here of which you can be proud.

Childhood memories come to mind when I think of nativities. Every Christmas, when my mother would pull out all the decorations, I would look forward to dusting off the ancient little nativity scene and placing it under the tree. It only had the three central figures; there were no shepherds, kings or even animals. The Holy Family was attached to the stable as one piece. It was made of some dark wood, unpainted, and the figures were carved—crudely carved, but

carved nonetheless. I would hold it in my lap and roll it over and over, peering into the stable to try to read the expressions on their simple little faces. I think I knew what it represented, but as a little boy, the full concept eluded me. Nevertheless, I was drawn to it and was filled with a sense of wonder. It remains one of my most vivid childhood memories.

How ironic that now, as an adult, I have carved a nativity of my own to share with you, the reader!

The elements of the nativity scene itself abound in symbolism. Mary and Joseph in adoration of the Holy Child provide the center of attention. The attendance of unearthly beings, angels, represents Heaven. Their very presence confirms the truth of the event. The three kings bearing gifts represent power and riches, the pride of man graciously submitting to humility. The shepherds, dumbfounded by what they have seen and heard, symbolize the humble, the common men of the world. The animals represent earthly creation, the natural world.

My nativity designs are decidedly more light-hearted than some, for they are designed with the folk art theme in mind. Still, I have tried to keep an air of reverence about the figures; their eyes are closed and their animals are at rest. Certain elements are repeated from figure to figure, such as facial structure and body posture. This is to provide a stylistic theme and also to help out beginners. As I mentioned before, all the animals are all seated. For one, they are much easier to carve in this manner. Secondly, they would dominate the scene if all were standing, especially the camel.

All the patterns are fairly simple shapes. In order to provide character to the carving, I rely less on the complexity of the shape and more on the detail carved into the surface. Depending on your skill level, you can apply as much or as little detail as you desire. With this thought in mind, beginners and intermediate carvers alike will find something of interest in this nativity. Several of the carvings in this book also require some basic assembly skills, as well as a bit of mixed media.

So carve away and put your heart into it! And in the true spirit of giving, present it to someone you care for. That's what it's all about, isn't it?

Getting Started

Wood Choice

Basswood is probably the most common and most popular of all carving woods. It holds great detail yet is soft enough to work without difficulty. Although basswood can be left natural, it is most often chosen when the finished carving is to be painted. This is because it contains almost no figure, or grain. Basswood is my wood of choice in this book.

You could also use white pine, a great whittling wood, but it has its limitations. White pine cannot hold a great amount of detail; small pieces tend to easily break off. Nevertheless, if you like working with it, adjust the pattern to suit your needs.

Butternut is an excellent carving wood and is fairly soft. This type of wood will hold great detail; however, care must be taken because some pieces can be quite brittle. Butternut has a very prominently figured grain. This combined with its rich caramel color makes for an attractive carving if left unpainted. If you choose to leave your nativity set in natural form, butternut is an excellent choice; simply finish it with satin polyurethane or give it an oil rubbing.

Although there are many excellent hardwoods for carving, such as black walnut and cherry, avoid using them for the projects in this book. They are extremely hard to carve with a knife and usually require the piece to be held in a vise instead of in the carver's hands. Other soft whittling woods, such as tupelo, willow, poplar and jelutong, are fine for carving the figures in this book.

Basswood can be found at most hardwood lumberyards. Another source is to order it from one of many available carving supply catalogs, although this is almost always the more expensive alternative. On the upside, you get what you pay for as carving supply stores usually carry high-quality wood. Probably the best source is to contact your local woodcarving club. If you are not a member, become one. Someone always seems to have a good, inexpensive source for basswood. Sometimes even free! It just goes to show how generous fellow woodcarvers can be.

Tools and Sharpening

With a vast array of tools on the market, it's hard to know where to begin. Start with the basics: a good carving knife, a v-tool, and two or three half-round gouges of varying sizes ($^1/_{16}$", $^1/_8$", and $^1/_4$"). If possible, have a good fishtail gouge on hand also. Over the years I have collected at least 70 gouges and countless knives. Is this necessary? Of course not, but there exists a specific tool that performs a specific job in any given project. It seems the more you carve, the more tools you find showing up in your toolbox. A carving can easily be completed with just a knife or two, but additional tools make certain cuts easier to perform, which speeds up your progress.

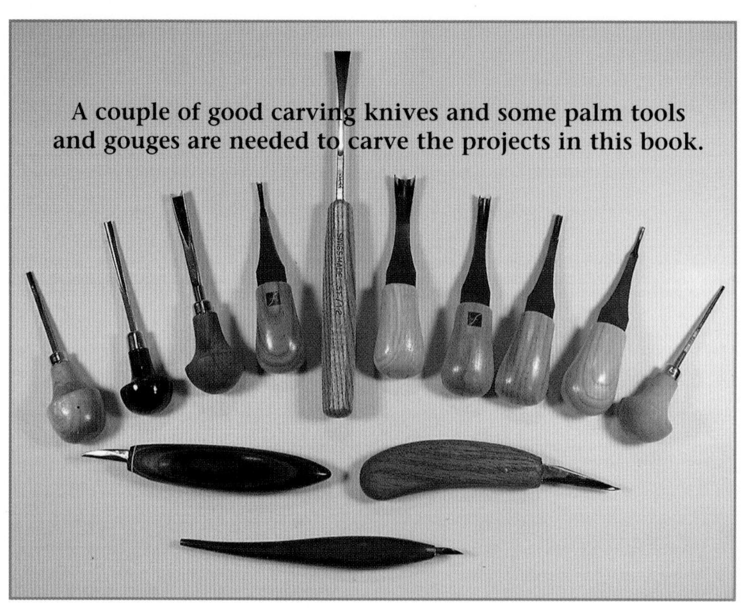
A couple of good carving knives and some palm tools and gouges are needed to carve the projects in this book.

As far as most of the projects in this book are concerned, the tool requirement is moderate. My personal course of action for small projects is as follows: Rough it out with a 2" knife, switch to a smaller knife to clean it up, then use small palm gouges for details. It is also very handy to have a fine detail knife in reach. There are lots of good knives on the market, but I am in the habit of making my own from either straight-razor blades or good steel from old snapped off pocketknives.

A sharp tool is essential. You'd think this goes without saying, but there are so many beginners who struggle with a piece of wood only to give up in frustration. They blame themselves, thinking they don't have what it takes, when all along a dull tool is the culprit. To carve with the sharpest of tools is a joy that must be experienced to be appreciated.

Learning to successfully sharpen carving tools is an art unto itself. It's practically half the battle when learning to carve. It took several years to become comfortable with my own sharpening skills, and I tried many different stones and accessories. I finally bought a motorized wet grinder. I get an edge fast, but I have to be careful not to end up with a little nub for a tool. Fortunately, you don't need one of these high-powered machines to do a good job. As a matter of fact, I prefer to sharpen my knives by hand; I only use the grinder for gouges. It would take a whole chapter or two to go over specifics, so I suggest purchasing a good sharpening book from your local or mail order carving supply store. However, these are the basic steps when sharpening a knife:

Using a good bench stone (I suggest a combination Japanese water stone with coarse and fine grits), remove any heel or bevel that the knife may have with the coarse grit. You want the blade to have two flat planes, like a wedge. For carving soft woods, like basswood, an angle of 15 or 20 degrees is required.

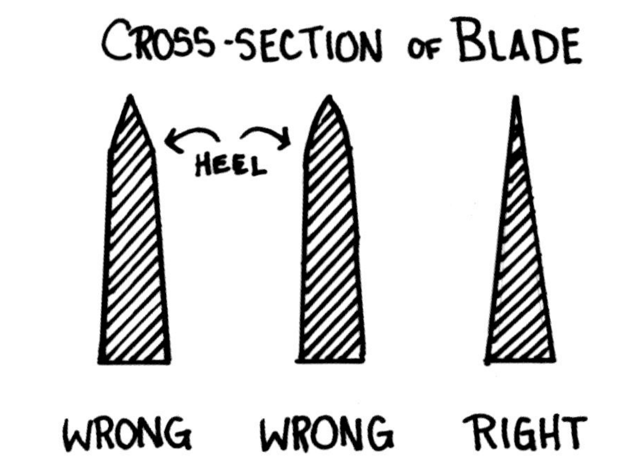

Notice the illustration. Using the fine grit, sharpen both sides equally, pushing the edge *toward* the abrasive until a small wire burr develops. Once you have the burr, you have gone as far as the stone can take you. Remove the wire burr by stropping. This is done by polishing the planes of the knife on a flat piece of leather charged with jeweler's rouge, or a similar substance. Be sure to pull the edge away from the surface this time. Stroke both sides equally until the burr is completely removed. This should leave you a nice sharp edge that is ready for use.

If you have sharpened your blade correctly, all you need to do to maintain the edge is to strop often. Plan to strop before each carving session and every 15 or 20 minutes during carving. The key is to never let your tool get dull. However, your edge will eventually round over from all the stropping, and then you will need to use the stone again. To test for sharpness, *carefully* place the edge of the knife on your fingernail and drag it lightly across. If it sticks, the blade is sharp. If it slides across easily, you need to sharpen the blade.

Remember, a sharp knife is a safe knife. Why? If a knife is dull, you will struggle more than necessary to make a cut in the wood, possibly slip, and cut yourself. When the blade is nice and sharp, it should glide through the wood easily. Of course, a sharp knife will easily glide through your finger as well, so it's a good idea to use some protection. A cut-resistant glove works well and is usually worn on the hand holding the carving. In the very least, use a thumb guard or latex coated thumb tape. Common sense helps. Whenever possible, keep your fingers out of the path of the intended cut. Apply pressure with the thumb of the hand opposite the carving hand to improve stability. Focus; don't carve in a distracting or poorly lit atmosphere.

Preparing Wood

You will want to photocopy the patterns from this book to use as templates. All the patterns in this book are actual size, so there is no need for enlargement. Of course, you could carve them any size you want: The sizes shown here make it easy to hold the pieces while carving. Just cut out the pattern and trace it onto the block of wood you have prepared, making sure that the front and side views are lined up. Also, be sure to lay out the pattern lengthwise with the grain. I have marked the dimensions required for each pattern.

You can then proceed to cut out the shape using a band saw or a coping saw. A

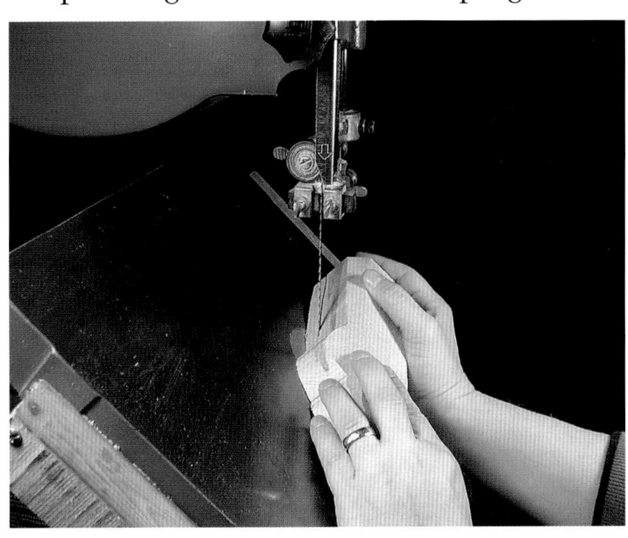

few words about coping saws. Unless you are a purist and are proficient with the use of a coping saw, don't bother. I have found a coping saw very difficult to use, and it can get frustrating when the saw drifts off course. The simpler patterns are extremely easy to band saw. Some of the others get a little more involved.

If you can, saw the front pattern first and leave the scrap sides whole. Then take masking tape and put the pieces back in place to re-form the whole block. This way, you can then saw the side pattern with stability. Remember to saw outside the lines, leaving about a 1/16" margin. This gives you a little play.

One last tip when sawing: it saves a lot of time to knock off the hard corners wherever possible. To do this, tilt your band saw table to 45° and carefully shave off the hard edges. Be careful not to pinch the blade during this procedure.

Basic Knife Cuts

Some of the basic knife cuts I use in this book are as follows:

Stop Cut This is usually a plunge cut made with the tip of the knife cutting directly into the surface of the wood. Wood is then removed up to that plunge cut, effectively stopping the knife from going any further. I use this cut to separate main shapes from each other.

Chip Cut This is a triangular geometric cut. The knife tip is plunged in on an angle three times (like a triangle), with the deepest parts of the cuts meeting together. The result is a three-sided chip popping out, leaving a matching hole. I use this cut to separate intersecting areas.

Scallop Cuts This cut is used to hollow out an area, to make it slightly concave. Lightly pare away the wood in the desired area, biting in and fluidly pulling out with a turn of the wrist. Take small bites, otherwise you may mar the burnished surface that the knife should leave.

Painting and Finishing

Every carver seems to have his own painting and finishing techniques that he swears by. I have tried several that I like and dislike. Eventually, personal experimentation leads to the method that suits you best. The method I will describe has been applied to all the carvings shown in this book.

I use acrylic paints as opposed to oils because they dry faster and are easier to clean up. The cheap craft types in the 1 ounce plastic bottles are great to use. They are inexpensive, quality paints, and there is a huge variety of colors to choose from, which virtually eliminates the need to mix colors. Acrylics dry very fast (five to six minutes) to a matte, not a glossy, finish.

Because you won't be spending much on paint, invest the money you

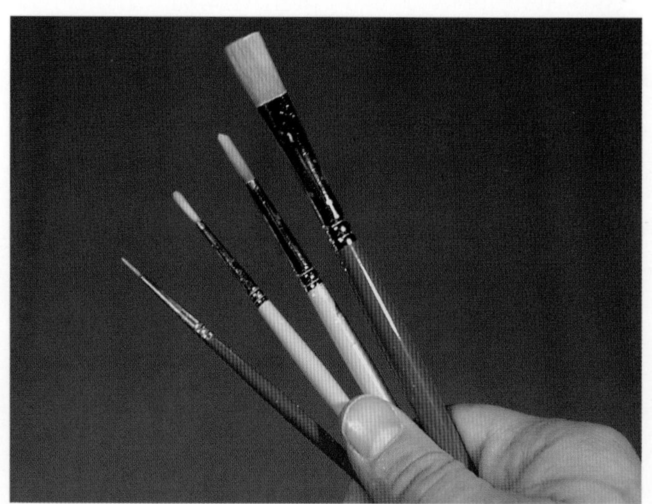

saved in good brushes. Really cheap brushes are very hard to work with, and they fall apart. I would suggest a high-quality synthetic or sable brush. You will want at least three sizes: a 1/2" flat brush for blocking in colors, a 1/4" round brush for getting into corners and some detailing, and a very small round brush for detailing. Make sure to always clean your brushes well after each use, especially when using acrylics.

When applying the paint to the wood, do not use the paint at full strength. Mix up a little wash on a palette (a baby jar lid works well) before applying it to your carving. I personally do not like my paints too washed out, though some carvers do. Don't be afraid to put it on strong, just be sure to temper it with a little water. This also helps the paint to flow onto the wood, as it is often rather thick.

When using white, off-white or yellow acrylics, I like to put the paint on almost full strength or to use several coats of a thinner wash. When using a metallic paint, like gold or silver, use it at full strength. If you don't, the shimmery effect will be lost. You'll also find that after acrylics dry, they will have a harsh, chalky look. This is okay; we'll take care of that next.

After the paint has dried for at least an hour, seal the carving with a high quality, fast-drying, satin polyurethane. Make sure you use satin, not gloss! It is important that you apply this finish as thinly as possible. I practically scrub it on with a disposable stain brush, working it into all the crevices. This will maintain the matte quality when the finish dries. This step is done for two reasons: 1) to brighten up the colors and, more importantly, 2) to seal the carving for antiquing. If you skip this step and try to antique the carving without sealing it first, you will end up with a big mess.

Let the carving dry overnight. When dry, the piece should still look matte. A dull sheen is okay. I like to antique my carvings. It pulls out the details and softens the pieces. To achieve this, I use an oil-based gel wood stain. Oil-based gel is good for two reasons. First, if your polyurethane got a little too thick somewhere and left a shine, the stain will help to dull that area a bit. Second, gel doesn't run. Whenever you use stain-gel or liquid stain there is always some excess left in the nooks and crannies. When left to dry, liquid stain will eventually run out a bit and leave a little brown run mark. Gel stays put.

The color of the stain is up to you. I prefer to use anything titled *antique oak, colonial* or *old oak*. These colors appear to be dark brown, but leave a warm, almost yellowed effect. Sometimes *fruitwood* is nice if you want an even more subtle effect.

Apply the stain with a disposable brush, working it into the deeper details. Slather it on! Then wipe it all off with a cotton rag. Make sure you do this immediately, as gel stain dries quickly. You want the effect to be subtle. If you leave the gel on more than a minute, you will have a hard time getting it back off. Let the wiped-off carving dry overnight, and your carving is complete. Be sure to dispose of your oily rags properly after use. Consult the safety precautions on the labels of your products.

Don't forget to sign your carvings! I usually carve my name in somewhere inconspicuously. I also use a permanent marker to sign and date the bottom of the piece.

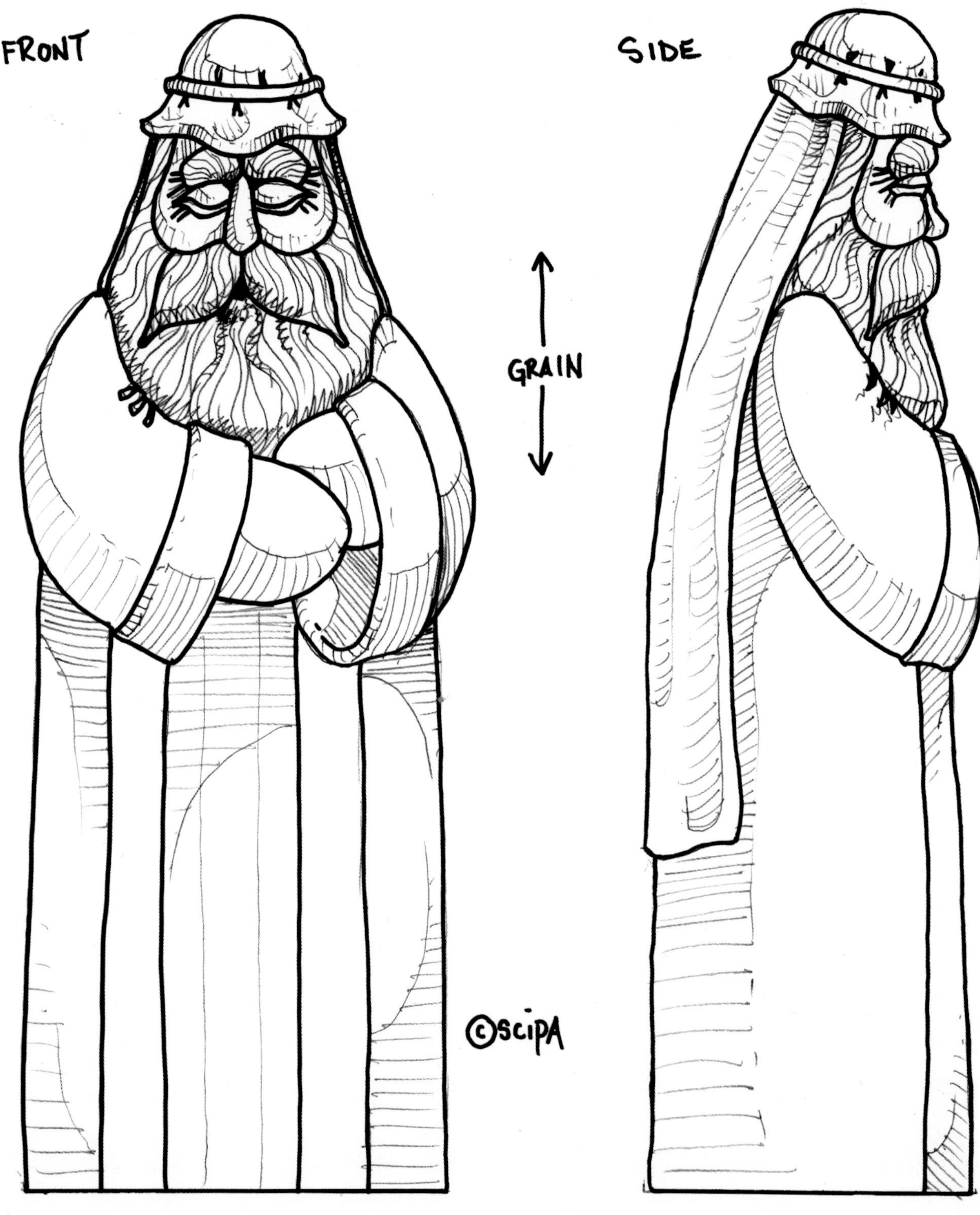
FRONT
SIDE
GRAIN
©SCIPA

JOSEPH

Patterns on Pages 8 and 10

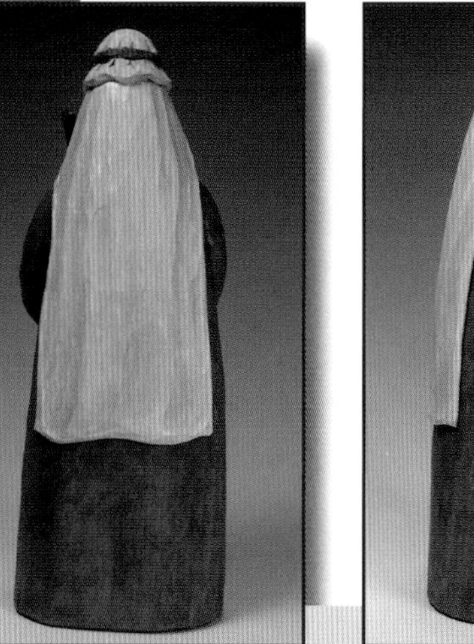

This design of Joseph is a good place to start the whole Nativity project. His shape is simple, which makes it easy to band-saw. You will need to implement basic carving techniques, such as whittling, stop cutting and chip cutting. You will also need to use v-tools and various gouges to create texture. This carving also requires simple assembly skills (the walking staff), as will several of the other carvings in this book.

The design elements of Joseph that you will learn in this lesson will help to complete some of the other carvings in the overall project, such as the shepherds and the three kings. Consider him a kind of template for the others.

If you choose to paint Joseph, I have outlined a color scheme to bring the carving to life. Of course, you may choose your own colors, or you may choose to leave him natural. If that is your desire, I would suggest two sealer coats of satin polyurethane. Once the carving has dried completely, lightly smooth out the finish with 0000 steel wool, so that it is silky to the touch. You may stop here; however, I prefer to antique it in the same manner as the painted carvings. It will help to pull out carved detail, as well as provide a rustic charm.

Your beginning block before sawing will need to measure 3 1/2" x 2 1/2" x 8". For the walking staff, you may use basswood, but I would suggest a different variety, such as black walnut or butternut. This would provide a nice contrast should you decide to go with a naturally finished piece. The blank must measure 1/4" X 1/4" x 7". You could also find a natural stick from the outdoors for an even different look; however, make sure it is fairly straight.

Take your time; don't try to finish Joseph all in one sitting. Have fun!

Materials List: Carving

Basswood block 3 1/2" x 2 1/2" x 8"

Walking staff,
species of your choice 1/4" x 1/4" x 7"

Larger bladed rough-out knife

Standard carving knife

Fine detail knife

#12 3/8" v-tool

#12 1/8" v-tool

#9 1/2" half round gouge

#11 1/8" half round gouge

#11 1/16" half-round gouge (veiner)

Pencil or fine marker

1/8" shallow gouge

Band saw

Carving glove or thumb tape
for protection

Materials List: Painting and Finishing

1/2" flat brush for large areas

1/4" round brush for smaller areas

1/8" round brush

Very fine detail brush

Cornflower blue

Blue-gray

Antique white

Raw sienna

Dark brown

Flesh tone

Bright red

Maroon

Mauve

Dark blue

Fast drying satin polyurethane

Brown gel wood stain

Disposable stain brush

Cotton rag

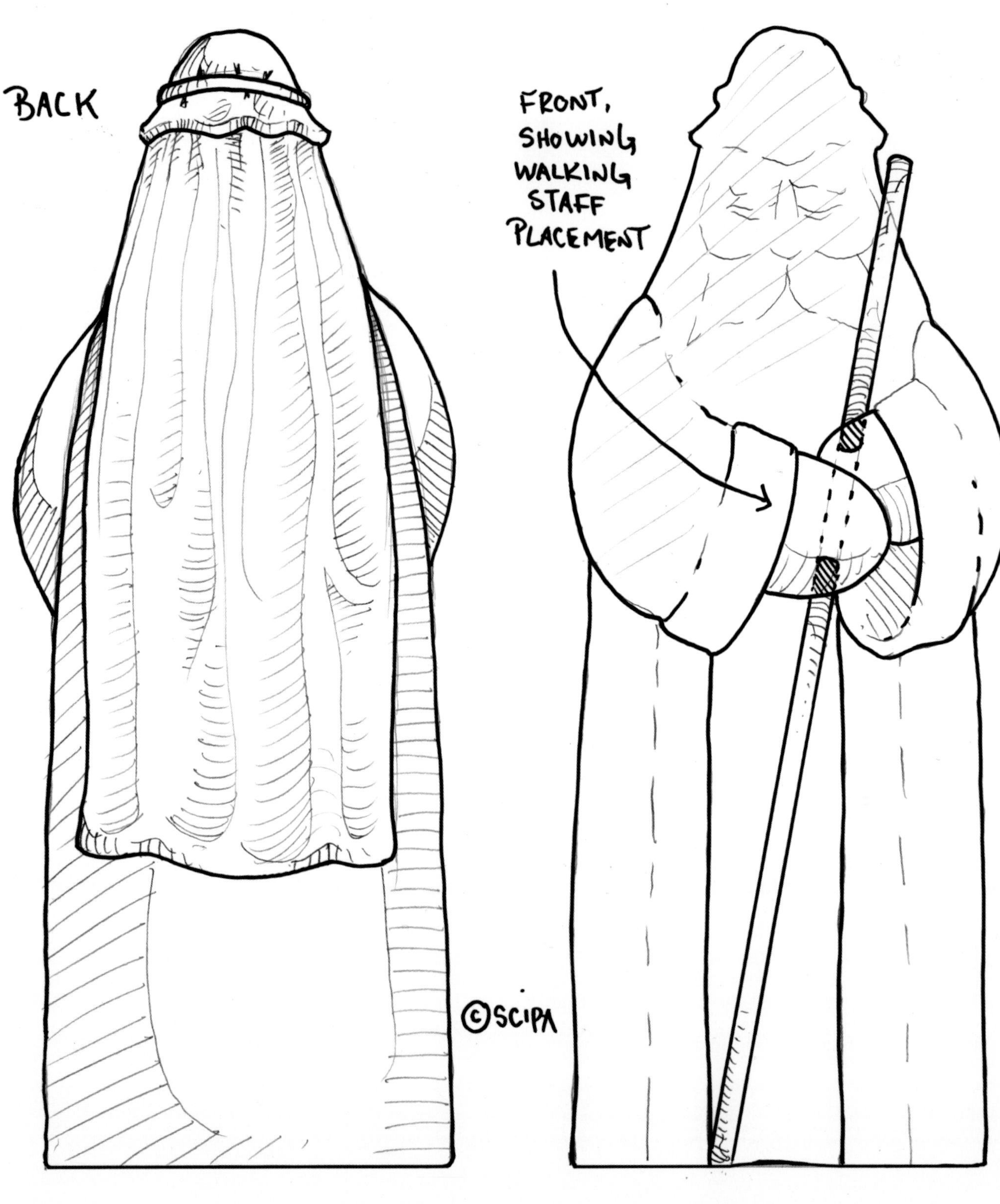

JOSEPH

Carve Joseph...

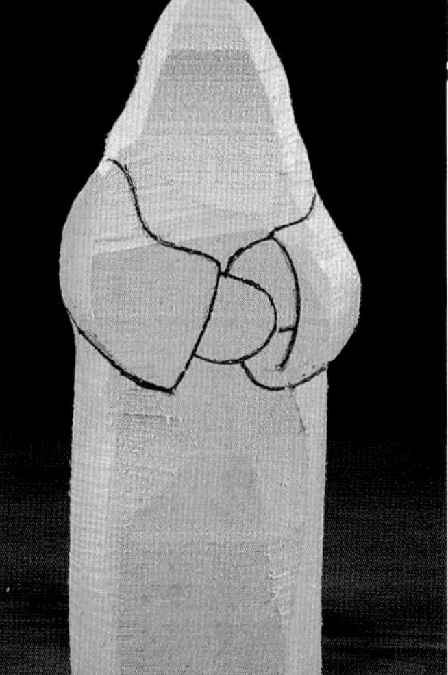

STEP 1

Read the section "Preparing Wood" in Chapter One. Using the pattern on pages 8 and 10 as a template, band-saw the blank. Sketch in where the arms will be. The prepared blank should look like this. (Shown is the front view.)

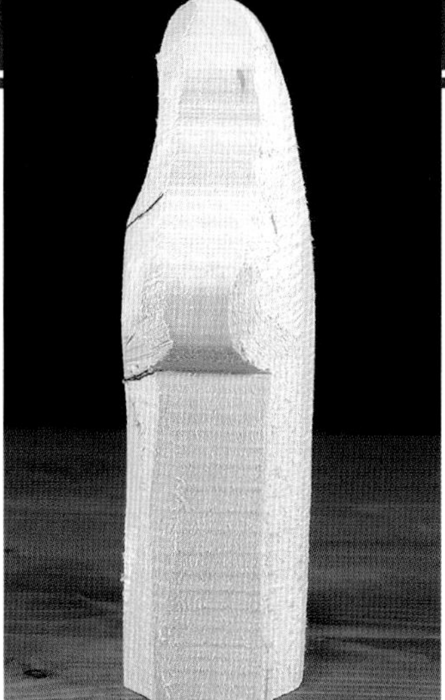

STEP 2

Here is the side view. Notice I have shaved the corners with the band saw. In order to avoid confusion throughout this lesson, when I refer to left and right, I am referring to *Joseph's* orientation, not the viewer's.

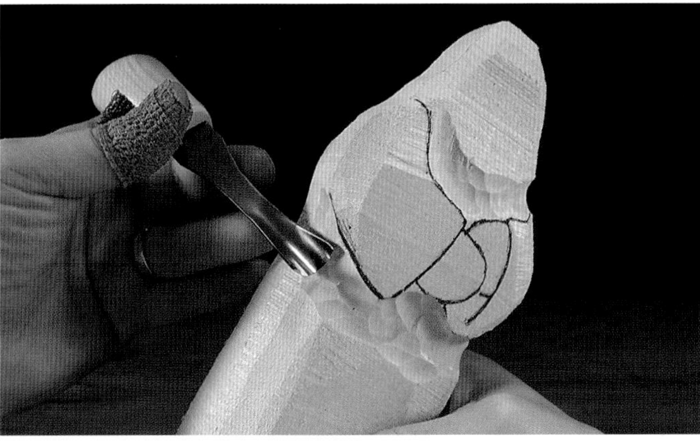

STEP 3

Using my 1/2" half-round gouge, I block out the bulge of the arms in the front.

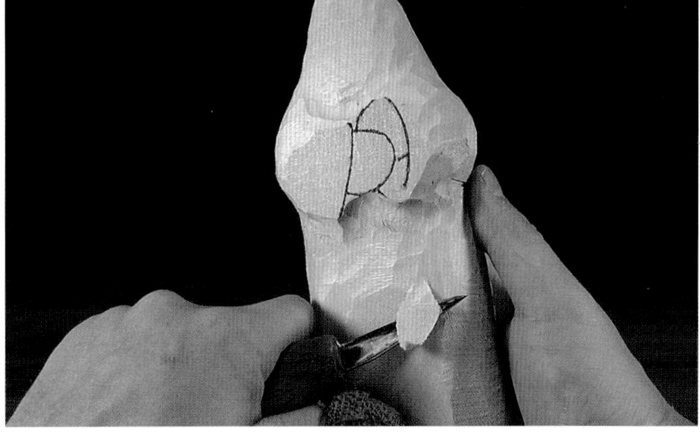

STEP 4

Using a rough-out knife, I knock off all corners and round out the entire body, making sure not to alter the general contour. This step helps to erase all the saw marks. Leave the hand area alone for now.

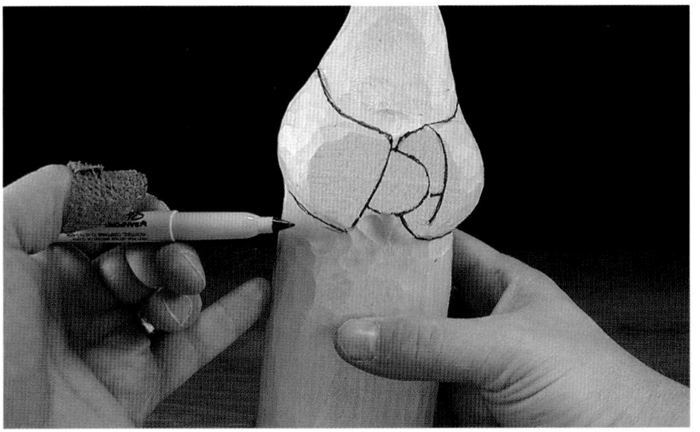

STEP 5

With the body now smoothed out, re-draw the arms. Notice that his right arm reaches over a little past center. Because of this, each arm will need to be carved slightly different from the other.

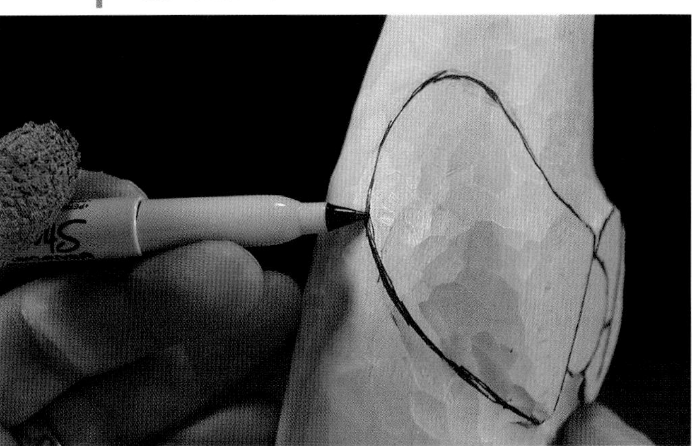

STEP 6

Shown is the right arm drawn in from the side. Refer to the pattern for this.

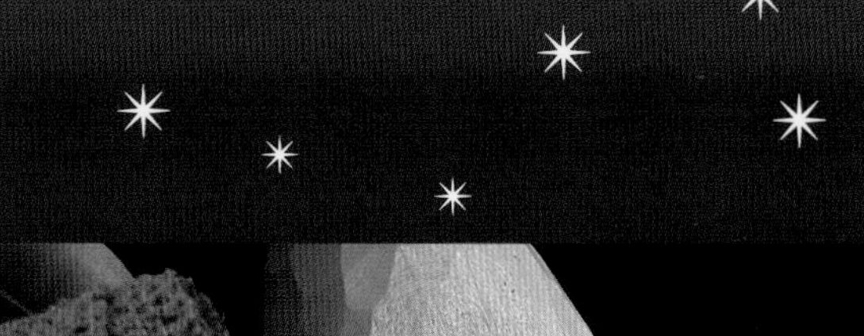

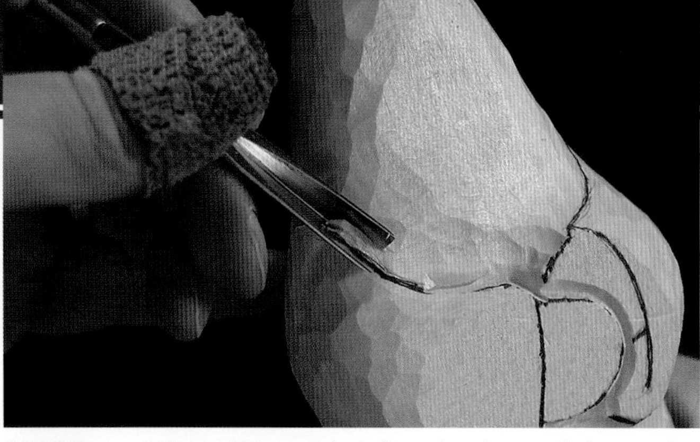

STEP 7 Using a 3/8" v-tool, define the shape of the arm by trenching out around the lines. Don't go too deep where the right hand overlaps the left.

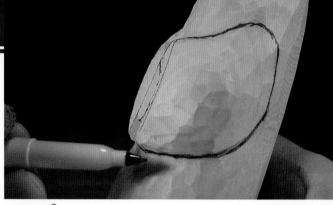

STEP 8 Next, draw in the left arm. This one is slightly more bent at the elbow than the other.

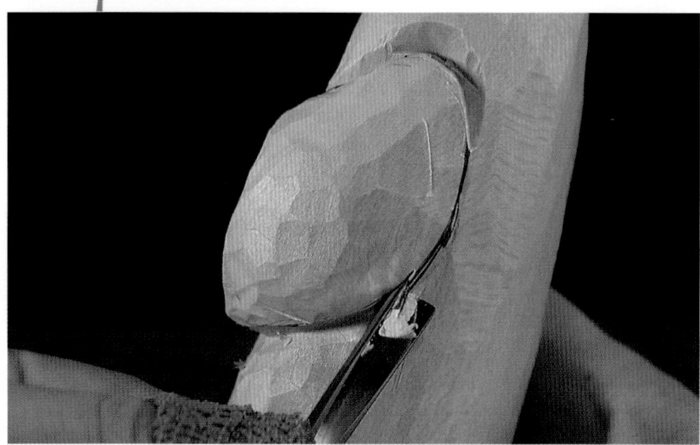

STEP 9 Trench out with the v-tool.

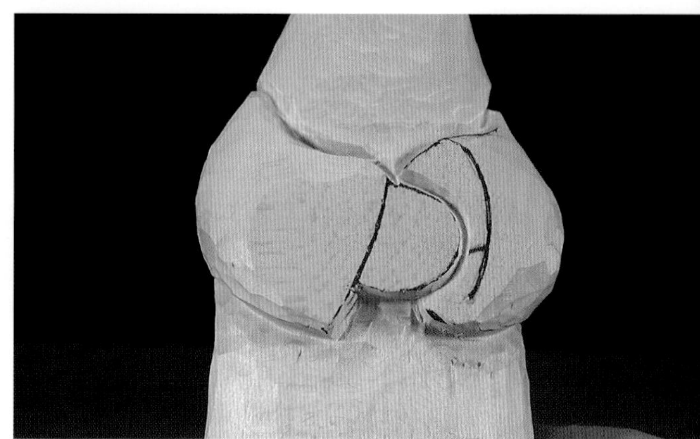

STEP 10 The arms are blocked out. Notice in the pattern how the sleeve of the right arm is closed while the left is open. Once properly carved, this will give the illusion of depth.

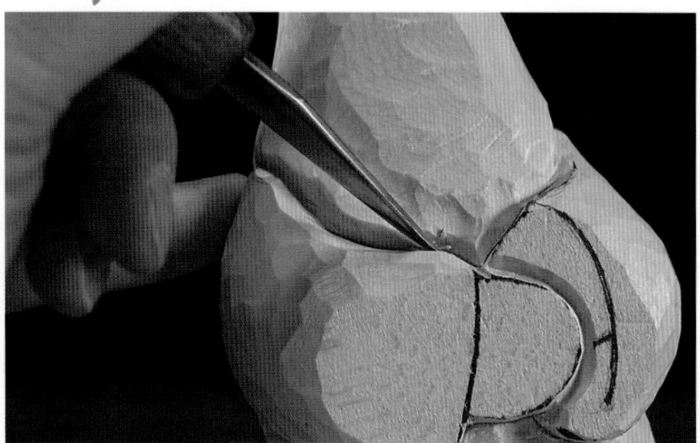

STEP 11 Using the rough-out knife, plunge into all the v-trenches to make stop cuts.

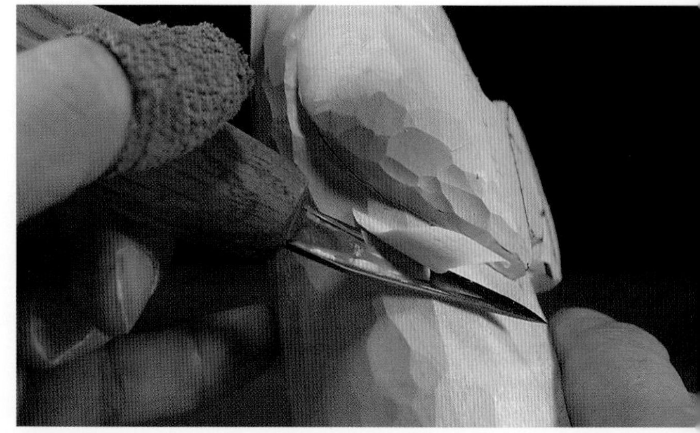

STEP 12 Remove excess wood by tapering up the body around the arms.

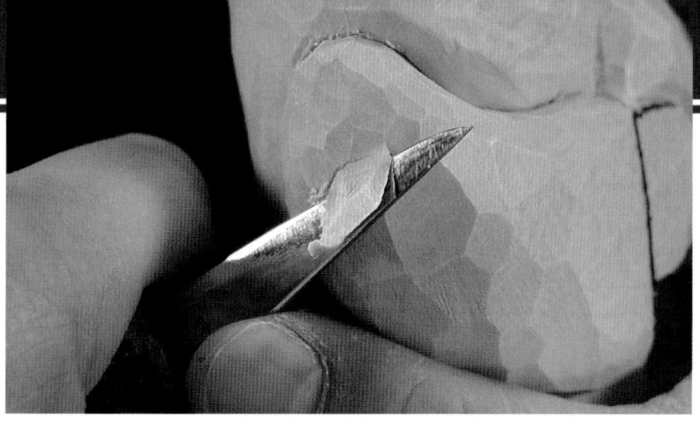

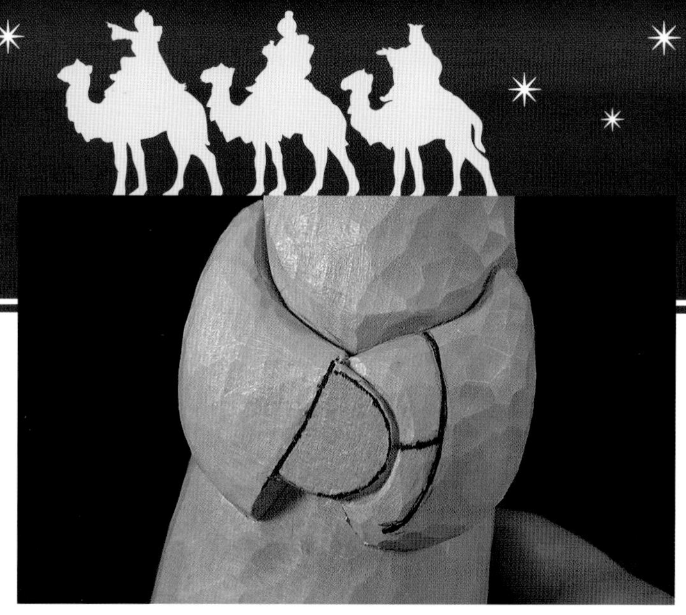

STEP 13 Round out and remove excess wood on the arms, to give them form.

STEP 14 The arms are now defined. Re-draw any hand lines you may have carved away.

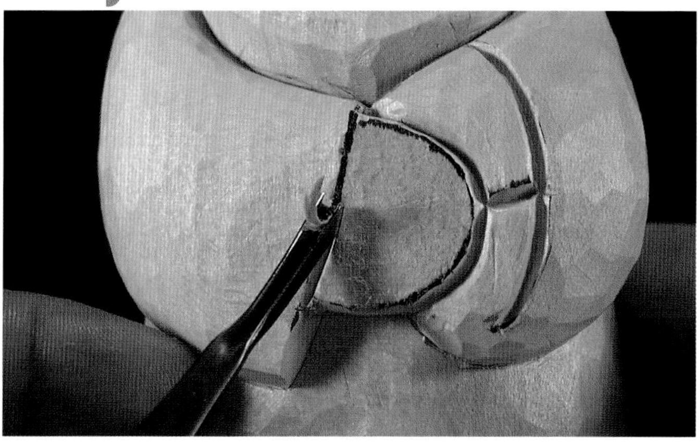

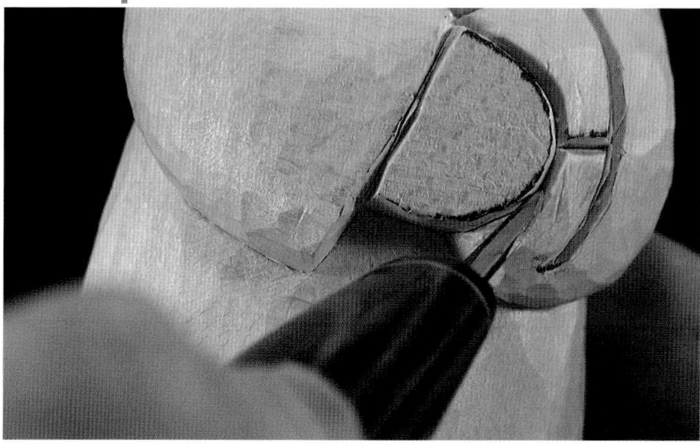

STEP 15 You're ready to work on the hands. Using a 1/8" v-tool, define both sleeves and the partially hidden left hand by trenching out shallow grooves.

STEP 16 Using a standard size knife, re-trace the v-cuts by plunging in stop cuts.

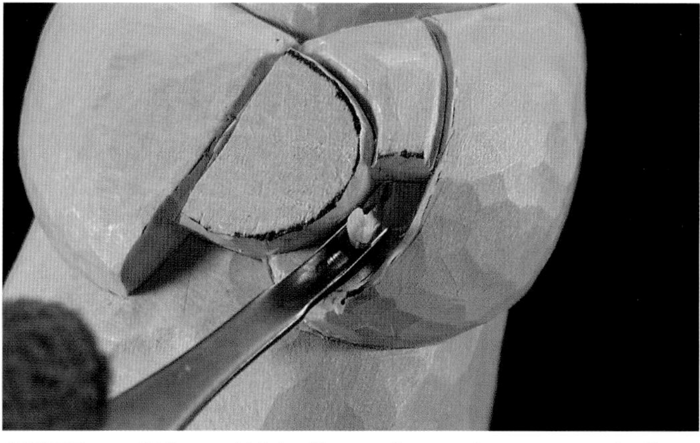

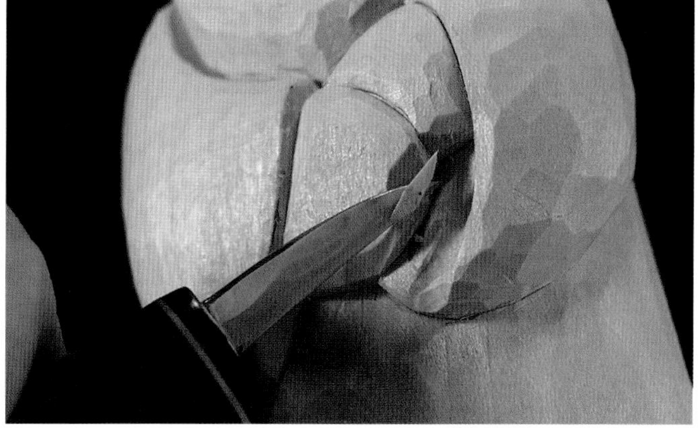

STEP 17 Using a 1/8" half-round, or veiner gouge, hollow out the inside of the left sleeve, as shown.

STEP 18 Using the knife, round and shape the hands. Make sure the right hand appears to overlap the left. I don't carve finger detail for this carving in order to achieve the simple folk style.

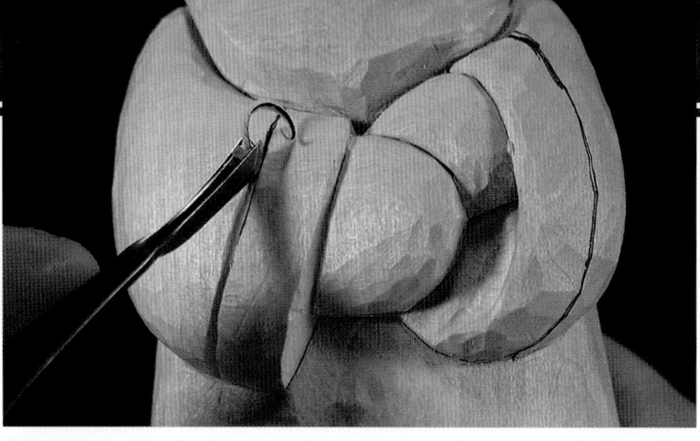

STEP 19 Referring to the pattern, draw and define the cuffs on each sleeve. You can use either a knife or a small v-tool to achieve this step.

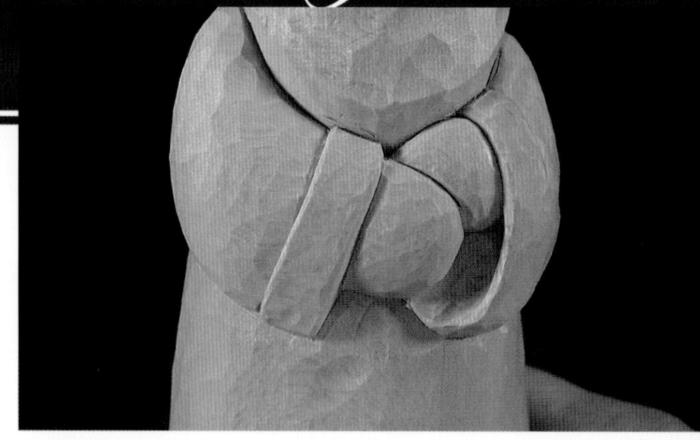

STEP 20 The completed arms and hands. Remember that a walking staff must still be inserted into the hands; this will be in the last steps.

STEP 21 Draw in the hems of Joseph's open robe, as shown. Make the opening about an inch wide.

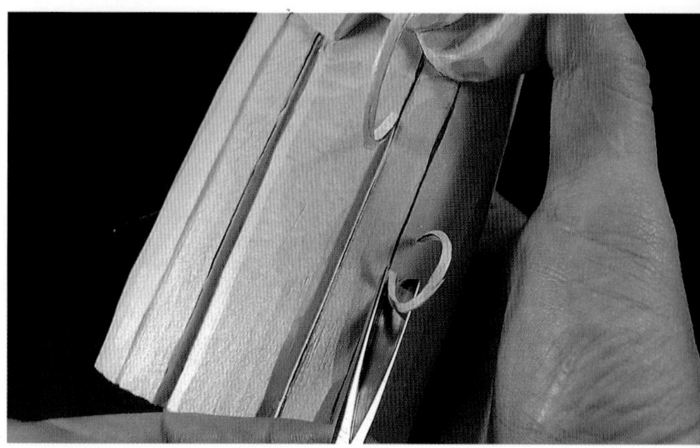

STEP 22 Using the $^{3}/_{8}$" v-tool, trench out the inner lines, going about a $^{1}/_{4}$" deep. Then define the hem by slightly trenching the outer lines, such as we did with the cuffs.

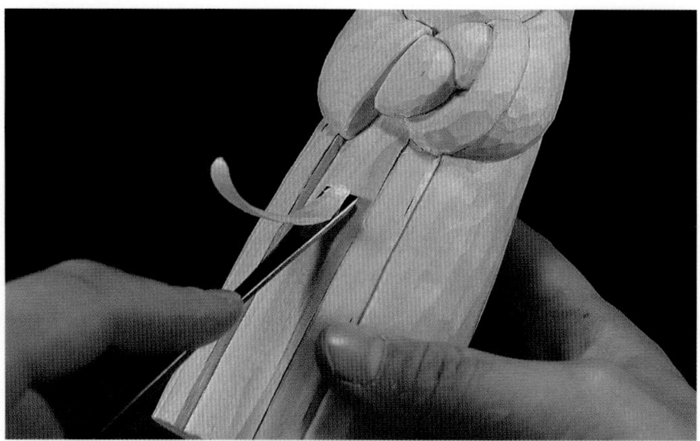

STEP 23 After applying stop cuts with the knife along the v-trenches, remove the excess wood to form the inner robe. I like to use a $^{1}/_{2}$" fishtail gouge for this step.

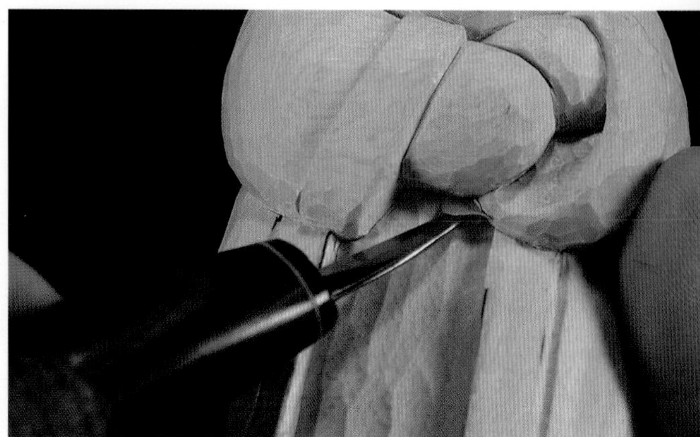

STEP 24 Clean up underneath the hands with the knife. Remember, the walking staff will be going here.

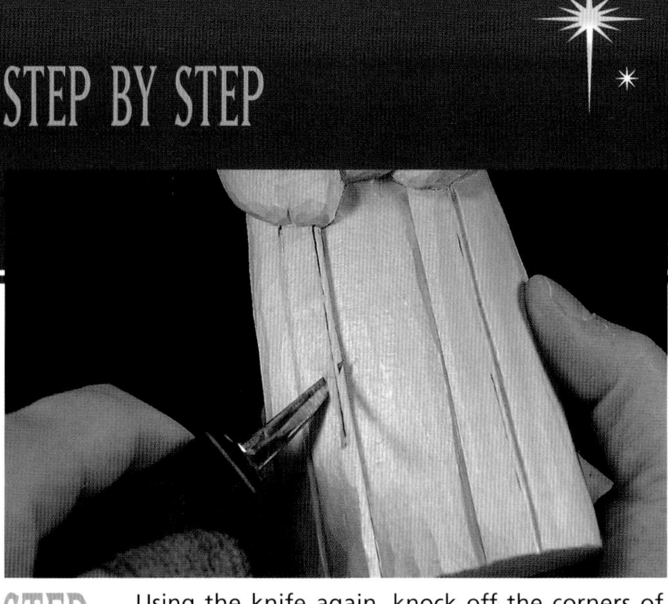

STEP 25 Using the knife again, knock off the corners of the hems and round them a little to finish.

STEP 26 Add two or three small narrow chip cuts with the knife to create crinkles in the fabric where the elbow bends, as shown.

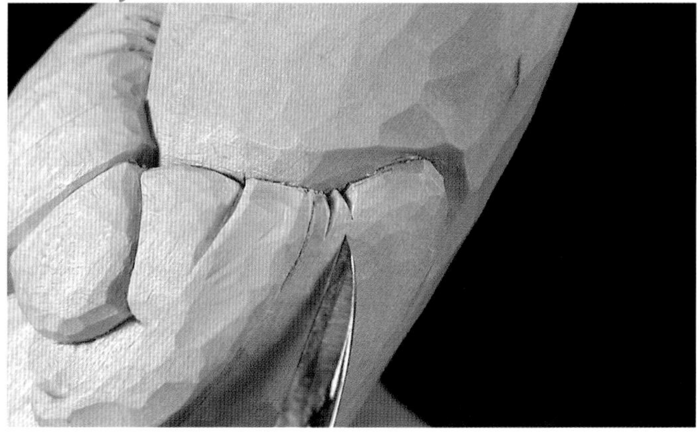

STEP 27 Do the other arm.

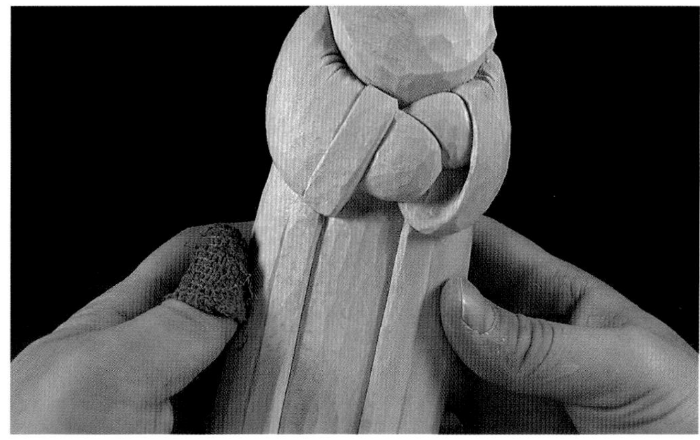

STEP 28 Progress so far. Other than adding the walking staff, the front body is complete.

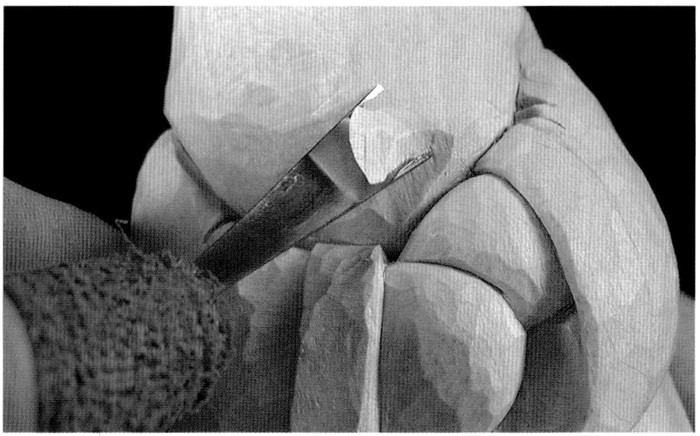

STEP 29 Move on to the head area. Using the fishtail gouge, cut back on the beard area by removing excess wood above the arms.

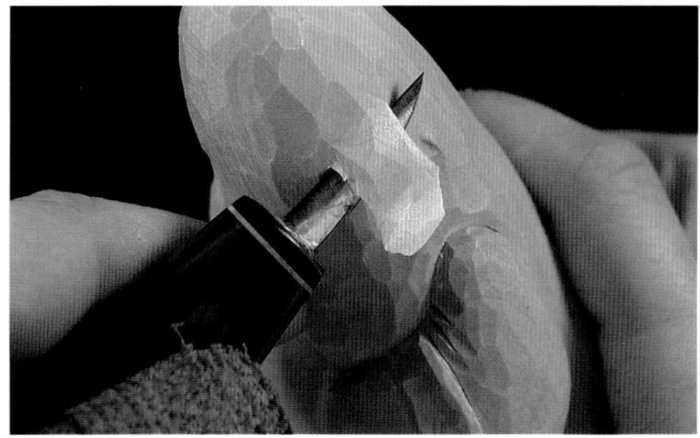

STEP 30 Referring to the pattern, re-shape the head by removing excess wood with the knife.

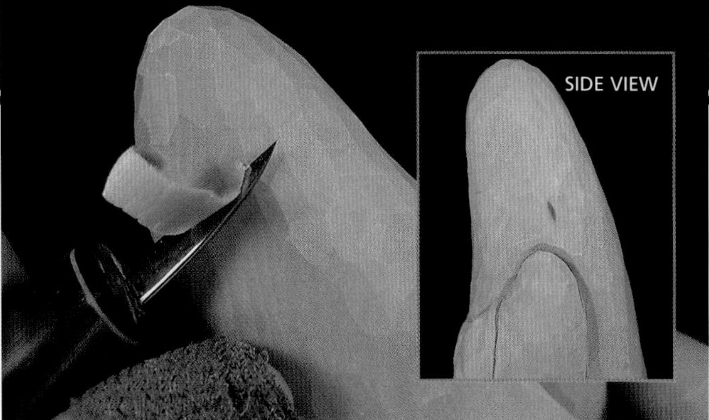

STEP 31 Remove excess wood on the back of the head, sloping towards the top. The profile should suggest a slight bowing of the head.

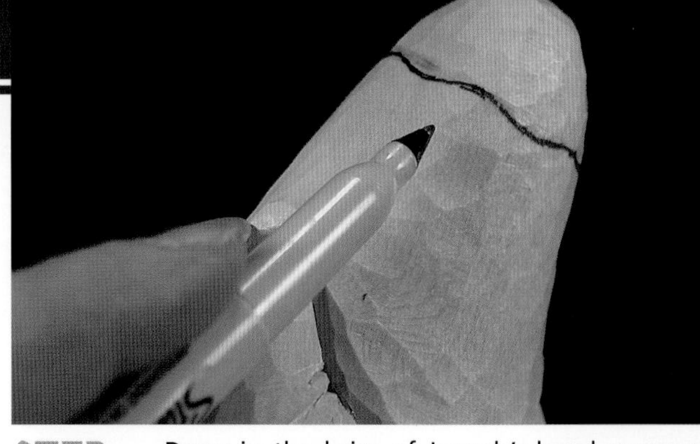

STEP 32 Draw in the brim of Joseph's head garment, or *gutra*. Be sure to make it slightly wavy to suggest floppiness. Also be sure to apply the correct angle in relation to the tilted head. Refer to the pattern for correct placement.

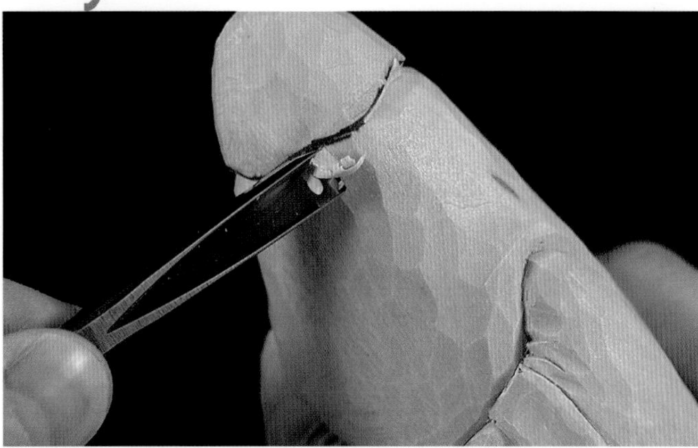

STEP 33 Using the 3/8" v-tool, separate the *gutra* from the head. Follow the wavy line and don't go too deep!

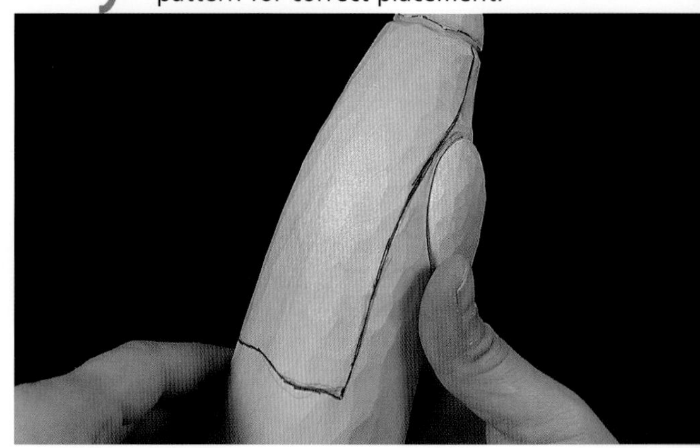

STEP 34 Draw in the long duster portion of the *gutra*. Refer to both the side and back views on the pattern pages for placement. Be sure to make the bottom edge a bit wavy.

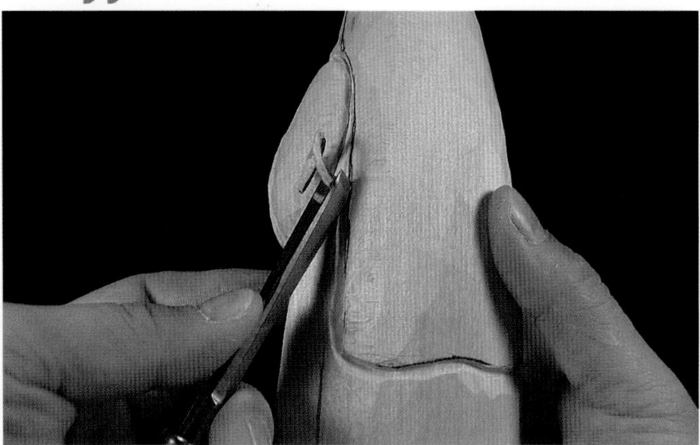

STEP 35 Using the 3/8" v-tool, trench out around to define the duster.

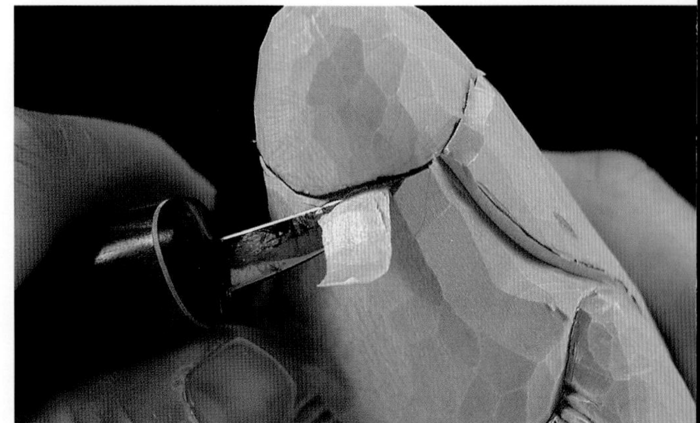

STEP 36 Using the knife, apply plunging stop cuts to all the v-trenches. Clean away excess wood from the face, sides, and back. Create the effect of the duster overlapping the exposed facial area, and in turn, the cap overlapping the duster.

STEP 37 It should look something like this. Notice the separation of all areas: cap, duster, face, as well as the arms.

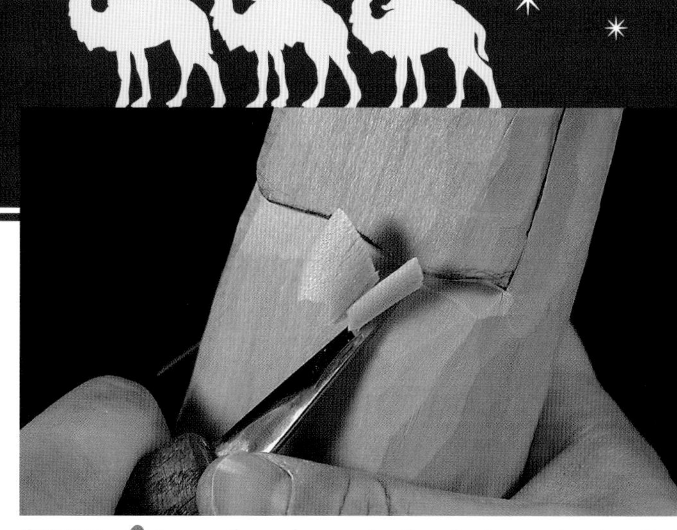

STEP 38 Taper the robe up to the duster, reshaping the sides and back of the main body. Again, give the effect of the duster overlapping the outer robe. I am using the rough-out knife here; you could also use the fishtail gouge for more texture.

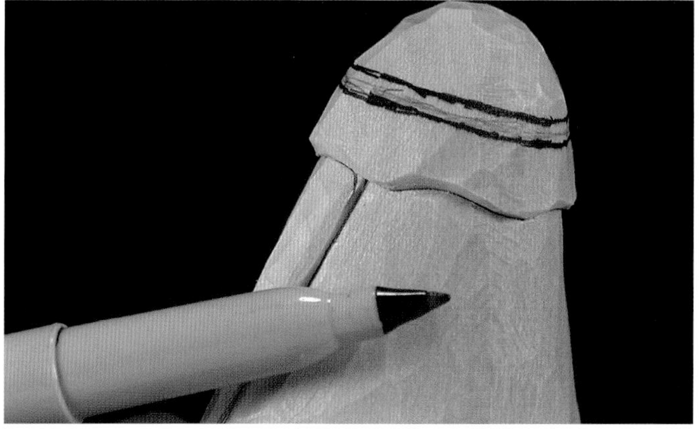

STEP 39 Draw in the head-band evenly spaced all around the crown of the head.

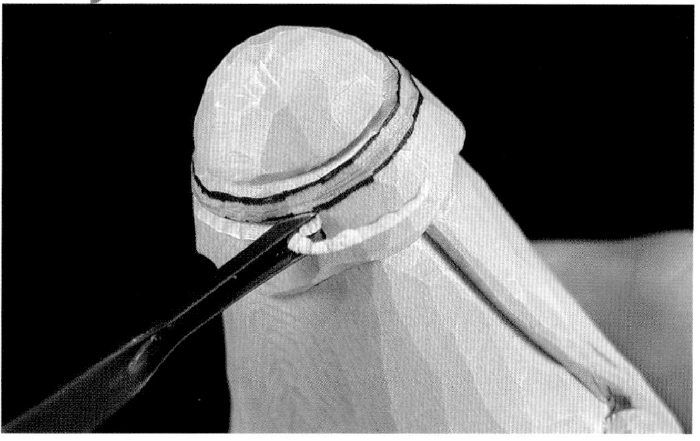

STEP 40 Using the 1/8" v-tool, separate the head-band from the *gutra*. Avoid going too deep.

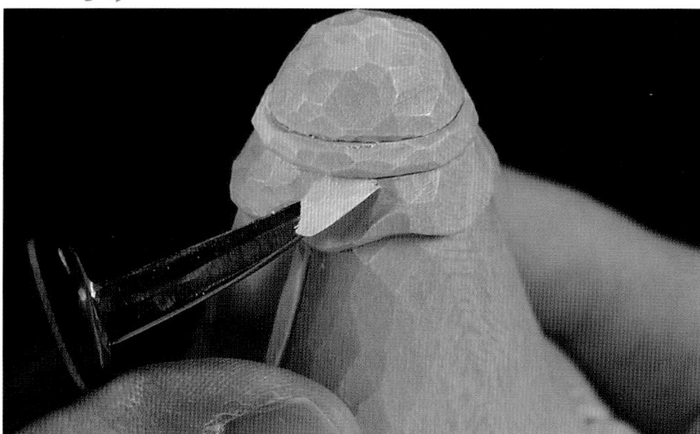

STEP 41 Come back with the standard size knife and clean it up. You may have to thin out the head-band as you round it and remove wood from above and below it. Scallop out small areas along the brim to further suggest floppiness of the fabric.

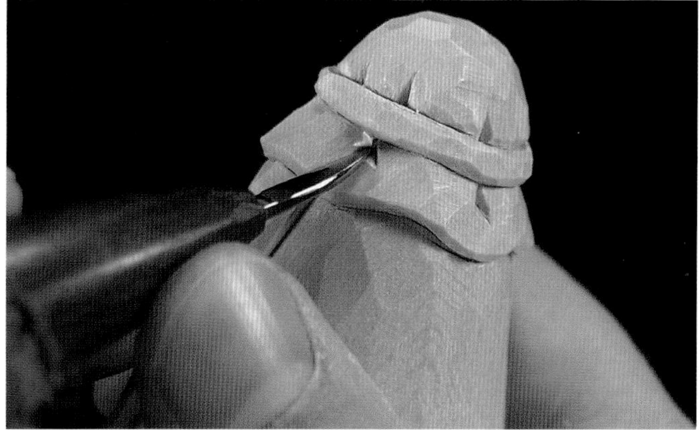

STEP 42 With a small detail knife, randomly place small triangular chip cuts around the head-band, as shown. This produces the puckering effect of the fabric being squeezed by the headband.

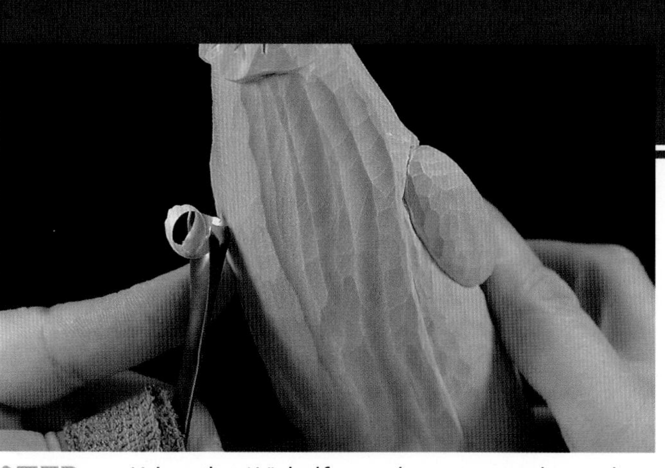

STEP 43 Using the $^{1}/_{2}$" half-round gouge, apply random scallop cuts vertically to the length of the duster. This step helps suggest draping of the fabric.

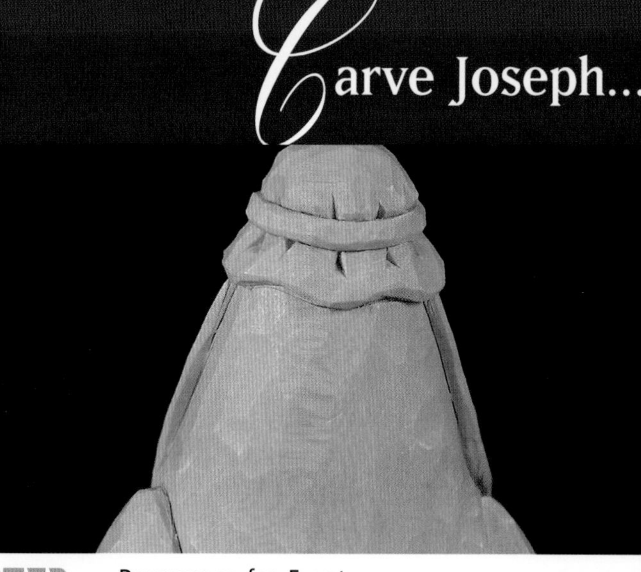

STEP 44 Progress so far. Front...

STEP 45 ...and back. The only thing left is to define the facial features.

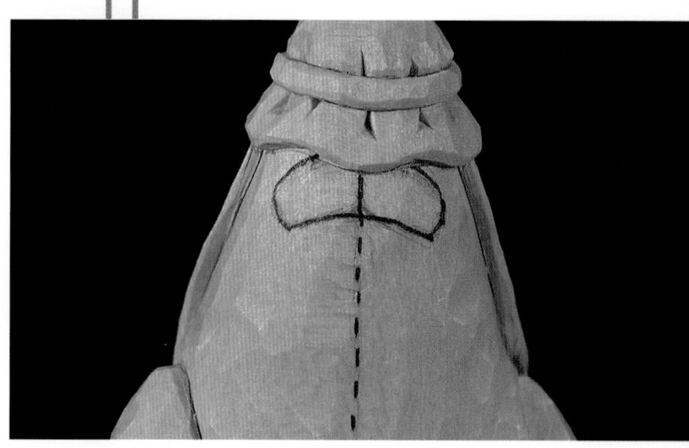

STEP 46 To begin the face, let's start with the eyebrows. After finding the center of the face, draw them in as shown. Notice how they are slightly hidden under the brim of the *gutra*.

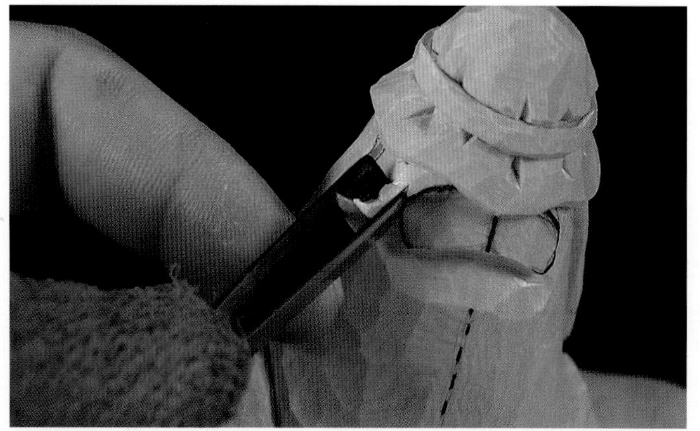

STEP 47 Using the $^{3}/_{8}$" v-tool, define the brows by trenching out around them. Be sure to tilt the tool away from the brows, so that a flat plane is formed on the surrounding face. Keep it very shallow!

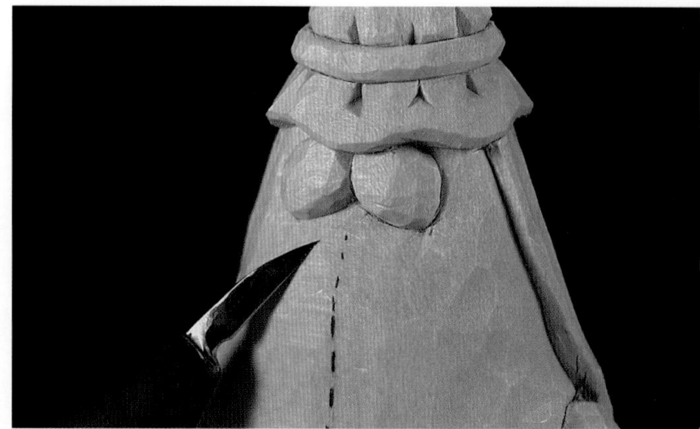

STEP 48 Using the small detail knife, part the brows and round them off. Also clean up the surrounding facial area, especially up under the brim. The results should look like this.

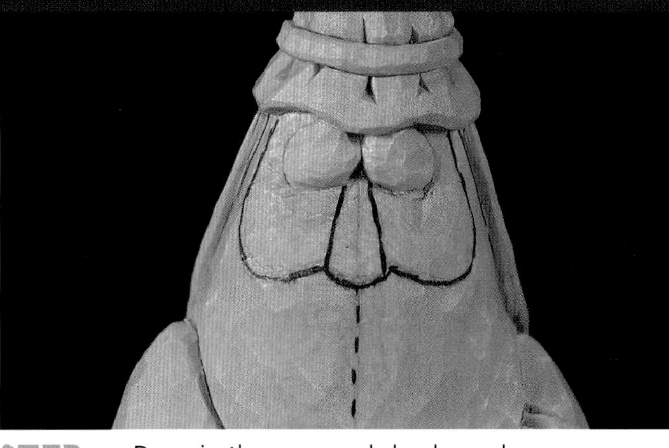

STEP 49 Draw in the nose and cheeks as shown.

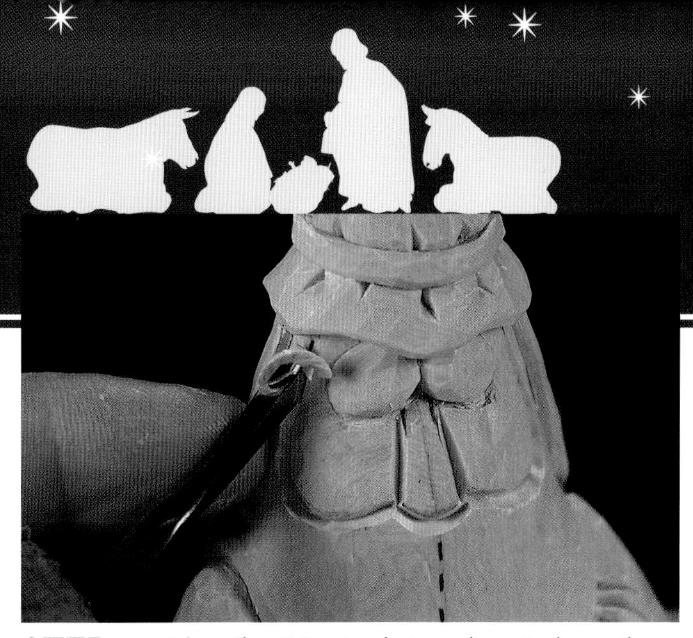

STEP 50 Using the 1/8" v-tool, trench out along these lines.

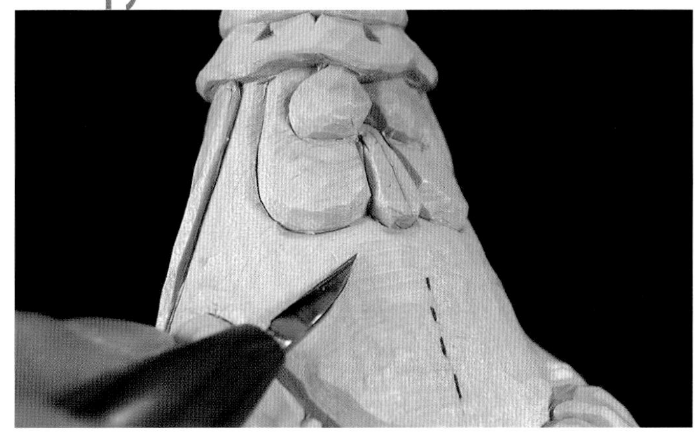

STEP 51 Using the detail knife, clean up the v-cuts by tapering the mustache area up to the cheek line. Further define the separation between the cheeks and nose ball.

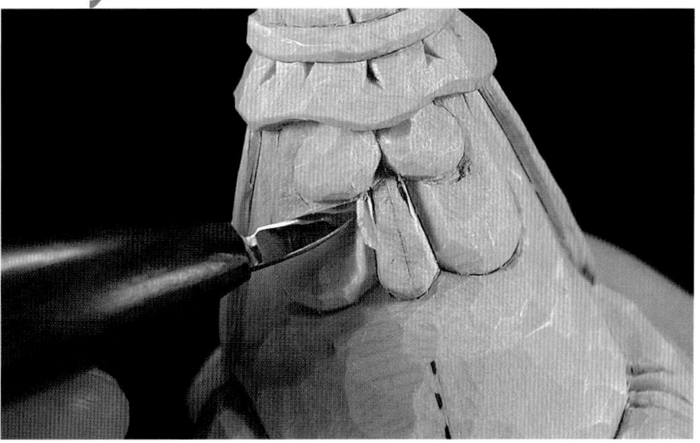

STEP 52 Carefully remove a small wedge at the cheek/nose line. Carry this cut through up to the brow. Do both sides.

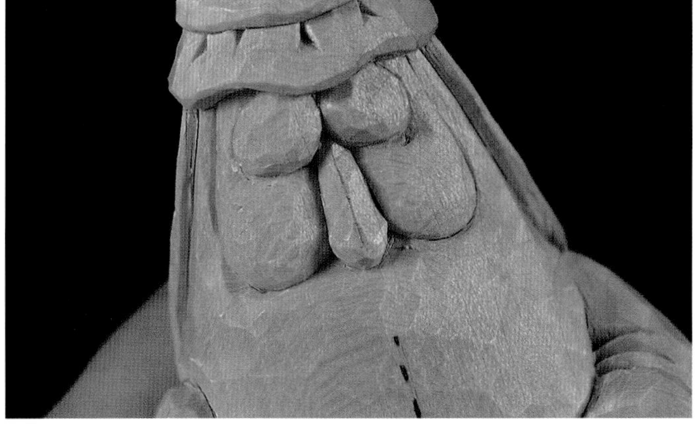

STEP 53 Use the knife to clean up the face by rounding the cheeks and nose. Taper the nose to create a raised bridge. The results should look something like this.

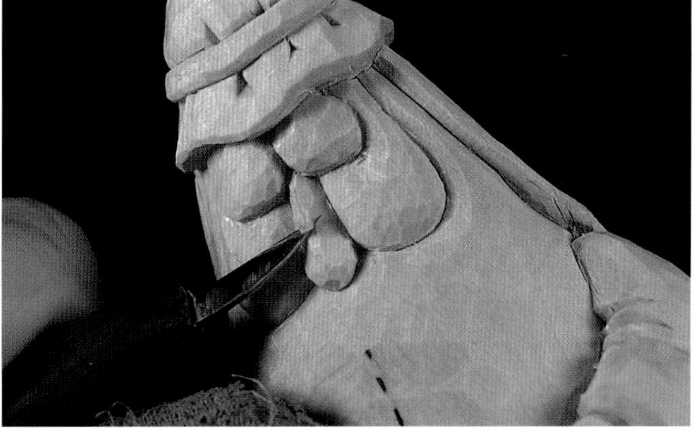

STEP 54 I like to scallop out a tiny amount of wood midway up the nose to provide some character. It creates a bony bump on the nose bridge.

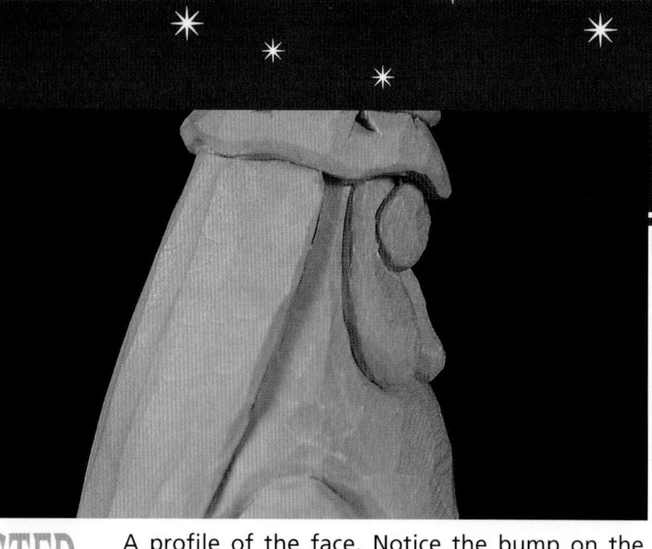

STEP 55 A profile of the face. Notice the bump on the bridge of the nose.

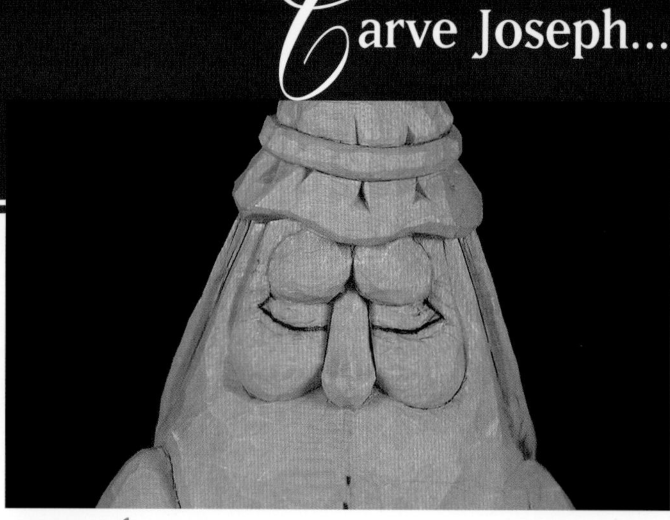

STEP 56 Now for the eyes. Joseph's eyes will be closed, or at least appearing to look downward. This means the most prominent feature will be the closed upper eyelid. Draw these in as shown.

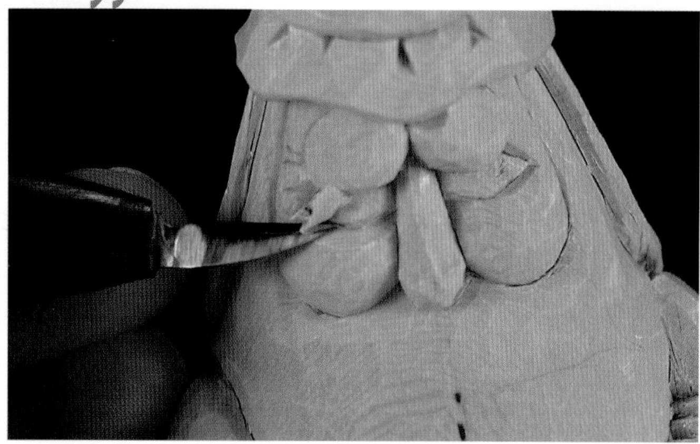

STEP 57 If you have not recently stropped your knife, do so now. Using the detail knife, define the eyelids. Using stop cuts, pare away tiny amounts of wood around them. Keep it clean and shallow. Do both eyes.

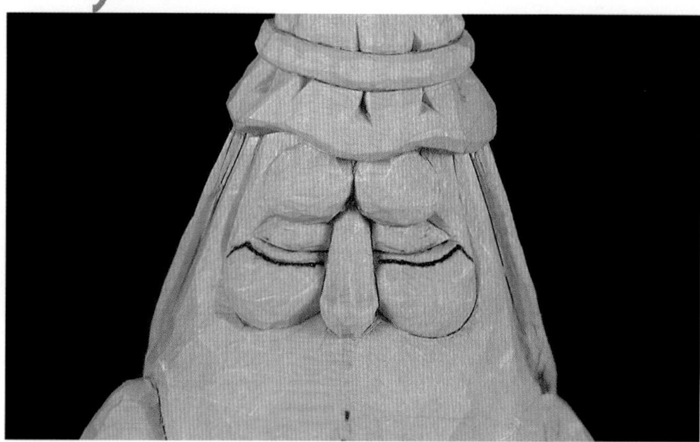

STEP 58 Draw in the bags under the lids, as shown.

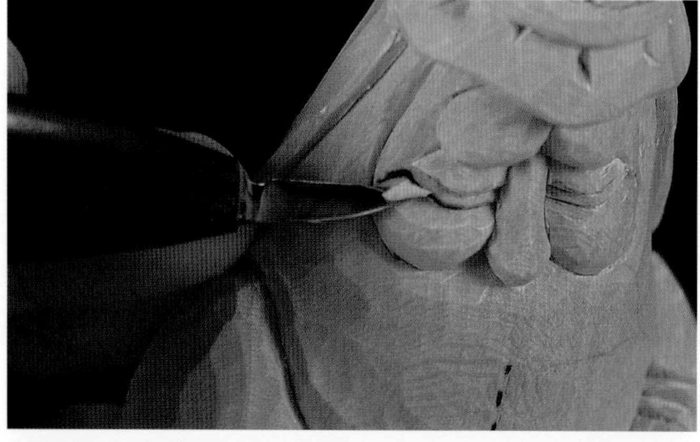

STEP 59 Define the eye bag with the detail knife. Once again, keep it clean and shallow. When removing the wood below the eye bag, round the cheek into its final shape.

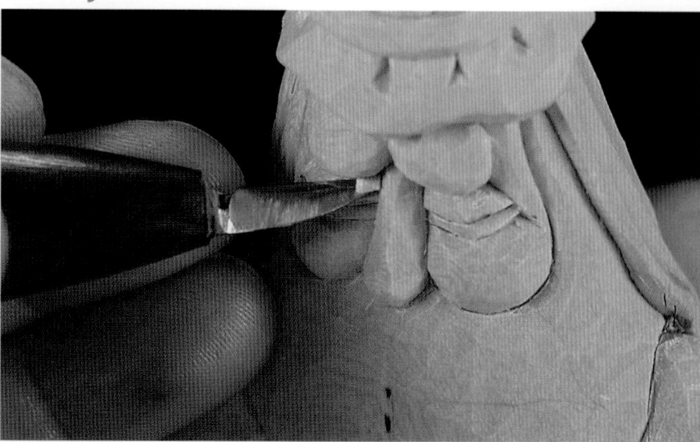

STEP 60 One more additional detail to help round the eyelid is to take out a tiny chip where the eyelid, bridge, and brow intersect. Do both eyes.

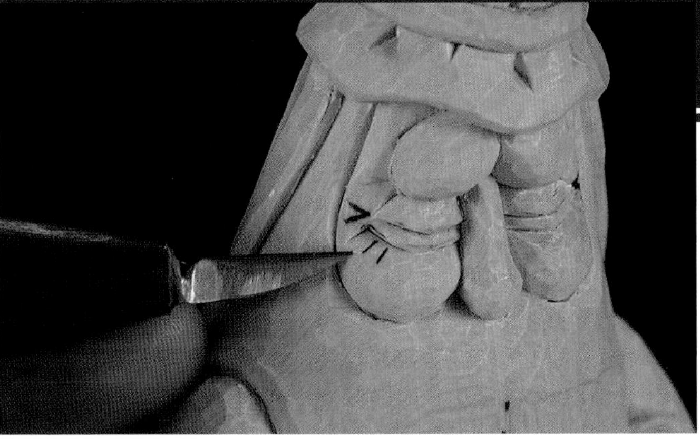

STEP 61 Final details of the eyes — crow's feet and wrinkles. Draw in as shown. A small chip cut extending out from the corner of the eyelid is sufficient. Two tiny v-cuts with the detail knife under the eye bags complete the effect.

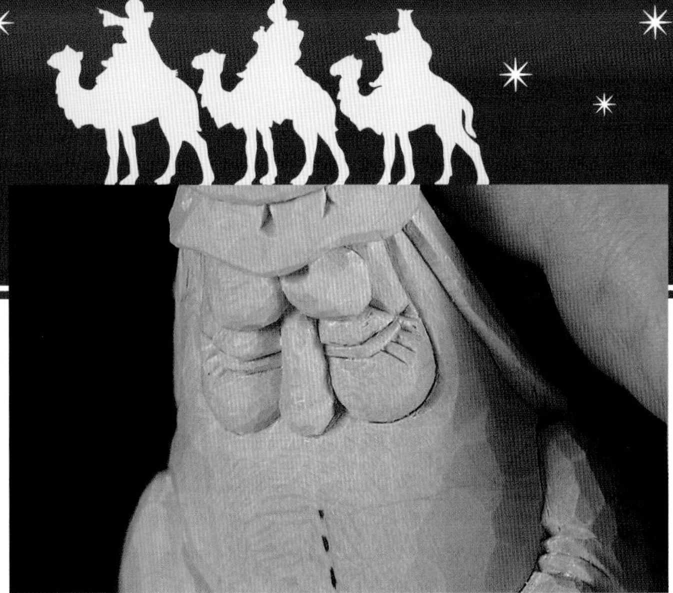

STEP 62 Progress so far. The face itself is complete. This is when you can clean up minute details or make adjustments to the shape of the nose, cheeks, or eyebrows.

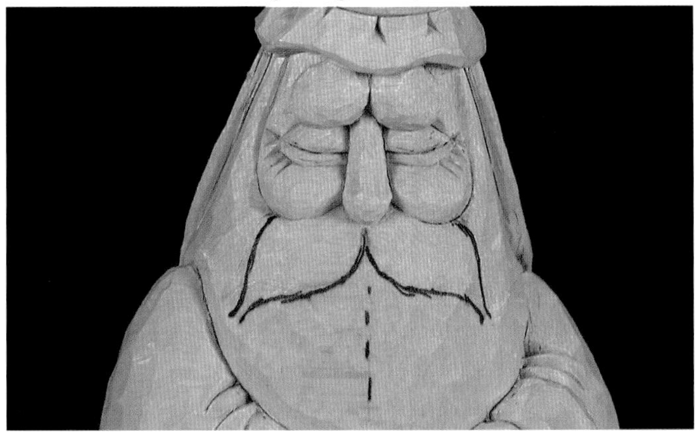

STEP 63 Draw in the shape of the mustache.

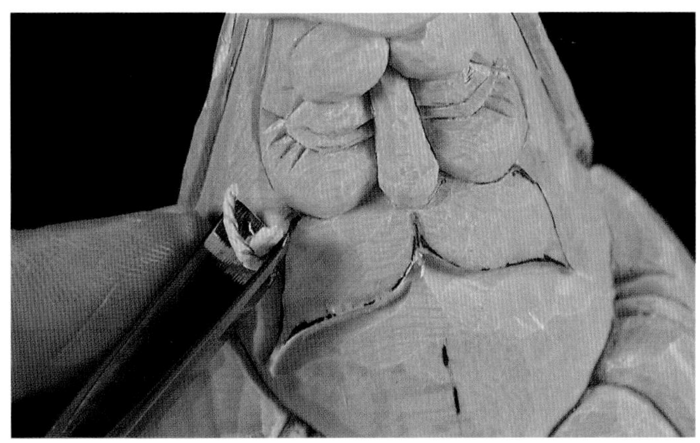

STEP 64 Using the 3/8" v-tool, trench out around the mustache.

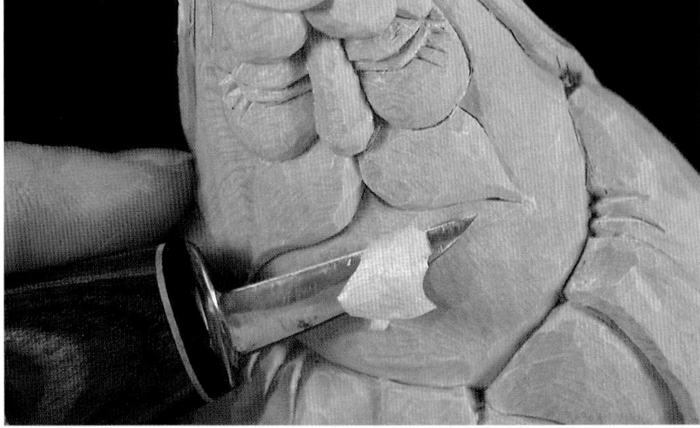

STEP 65 With the standard knife, clean up the v-cut by rounding off the hard edges and tapering the beard. Also define the center division of the mustache.

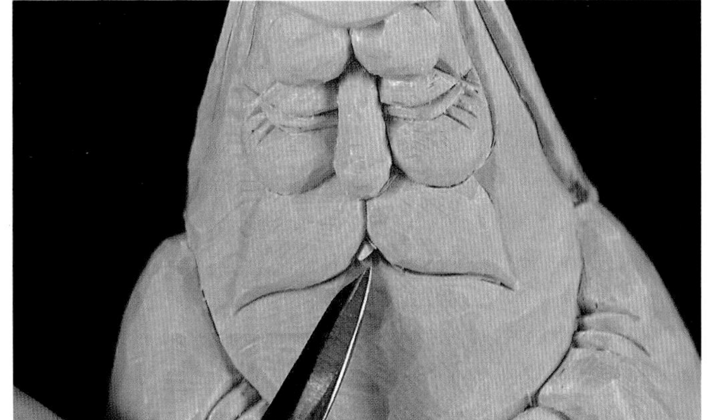

STEP 66 Take out a small chip indicating the opening of the mouth. I do not carve an actual lower lip on Joseph. You can shape the area a little with the knife to suggest one. This makes him look woollier in the beard.

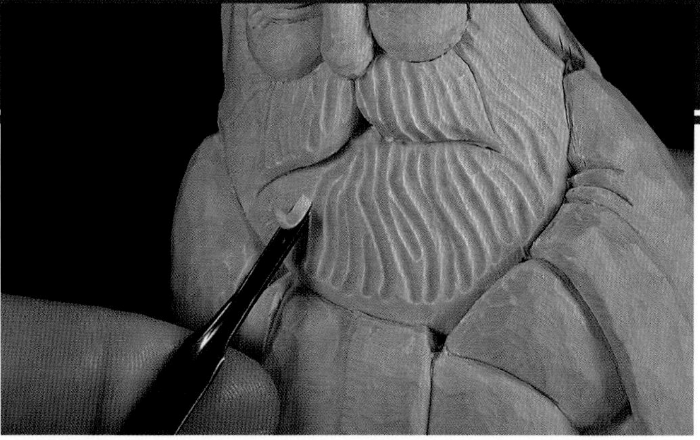

STEP 67 Texture the mustache, beard, and eyebrows using a small $^1/_{16}$" veiner tool. Avoid straight cuts! Instead, make them wavy and intersecting each other.

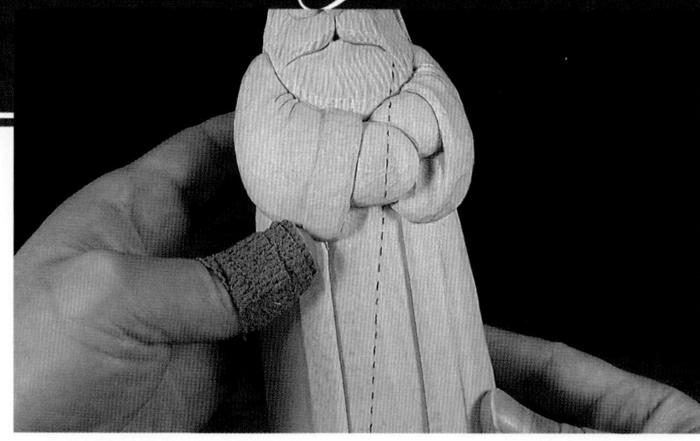

STEP 68 The carving is complete, except for Joseph's walking staff. I have drawn in a dotted line indicating its position. Since it will be impossible to drill a hole through his hands, two separate pieces will be inserted into shallow holes to appear as one piece.

STEP 69 For the staff, you can either find a natural twig or carve one, as I am here. I have chosen black walnut for the natural brown color. The staff blank measures $^1/_4$" thick and is 7" long. Round the corners with the knife. Remember, you will cut this into two pieces.

STEP 70 To make the holes for the staff, use a small $^1/_8$" shallow gouge to hand drill a hole at least a $^1/_4$" deep. Do the bottom hole first. It is very important to keep it in line with the dotted mark. Watch the angle - try to drill parallel with the body, not into it.

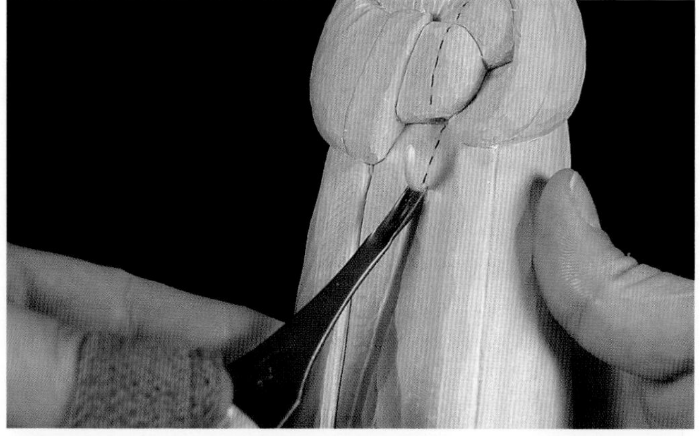

STEP 71 You will probably have to hollow a shallow path for the lower portion of the staff. Use the $^1/_8$" half-round gouge for this. Do a little at a time.

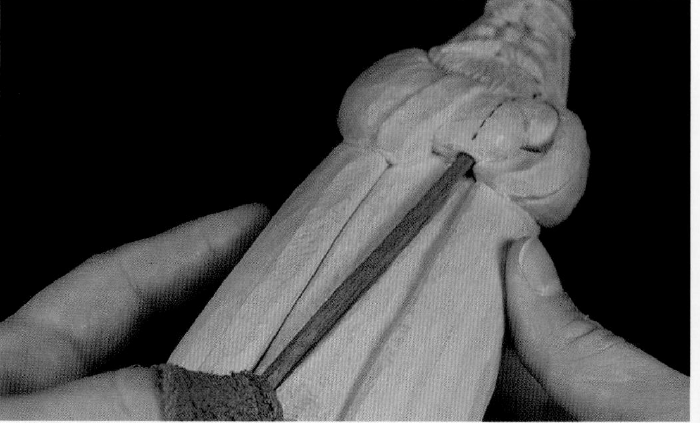

STEP 72 Cut the staff to length, and dry-fit until it lies correctly. Glue in later.

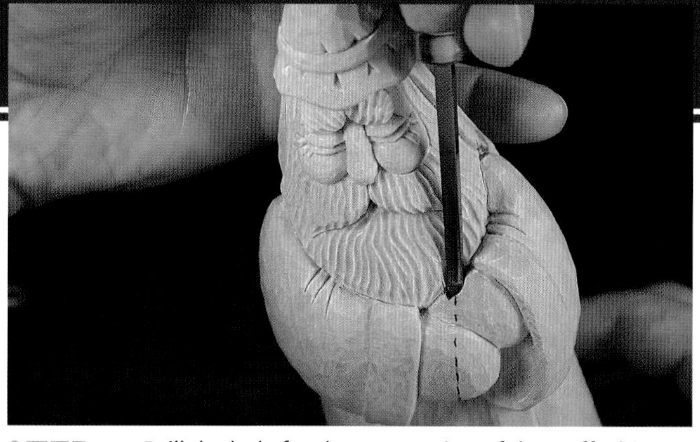

STEP 73 Drill the hole for the top portion of the staff. This can be tricky; make sure you maintain the angle, not only from the front, but from the side as well. Go about ½" deep; this will be the top staff's only support.

STEP 74 Dry-fit both pieces. Notice how it looks like one whole piece. Even from the side.

STEP 75 Glue staff in place and leave overnight. Rubber bands help to keep the lower portion in place while drying. Joseph is now ready for painting!

Painting Joseph

STEP 1 Before painting, lightly clean the carving with mild dishwashing soap and a toothbrush. This helps to remove oils from your hands. After it has dried, pencil in a few light vertical guidelines on Joseph's inner robe.

STEP 2 Starting with the outer robe, apply cornflower blue with a large flat brush. Use a smaller round brush to get into tight areas, as you need to.

STEP 3 Using the smaller round brush, apply blue-gray to the robe's trim.

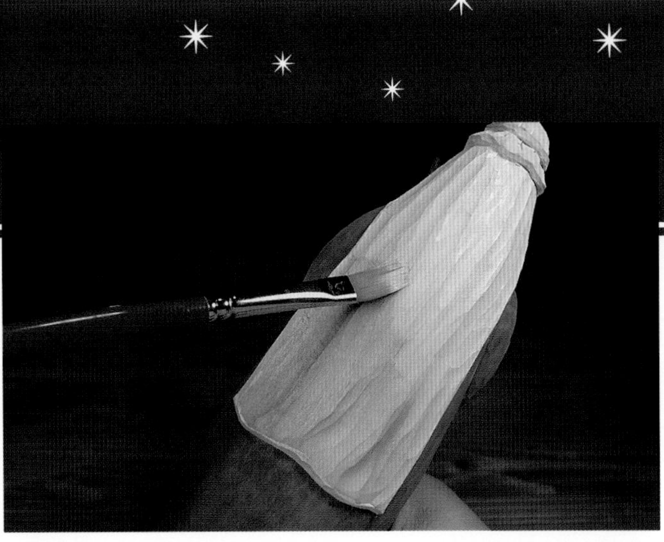

STEP 4 Using antique white, paint Joseph's head garment with the larger brush, switching to the smaller brush for tight areas. I prefer to apply white a little thicker, or in two coats. This is to ensure that the antiquing will not overwhelm the white.

STEP 5 For the beard, hair, and eyebrows, use a thin wash of raw sienna. Use the small round brush.

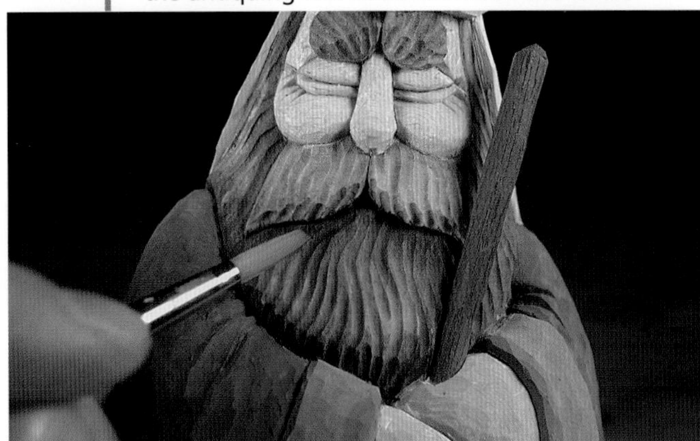

STEP 6 I like to give the hair and beard a little extra dimension. To do this, apply a bit of washed out dark brown into the edges and deeper areas. Blend it in with water, creating lowlights.

STEP 7 Third, apply a thin wash of the raw sienna mixed with antique white to the high points of the beard and hair, creating highlights. The subtleties may not be so obvious in these photos, but they do make a difference in real life, especially when the sealer coat is applied.

STEP 8 Using the small round brush, apply flesh tone to the face and hands.

STEP 9 Mix a little bright red with the flesh tone and apply to the cheeks for a rosy glow. Also apply a bit to the eyelids and the deep areas of the hands. Be sure to blend it in!

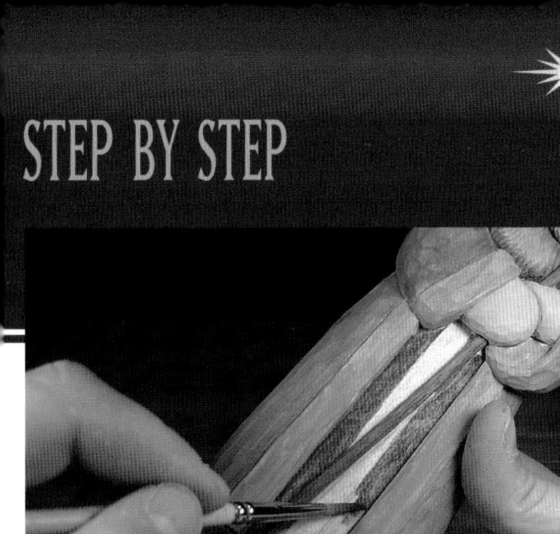

STEP 10 Using the small round brush, apply maroon to the headband and to the two outer stripes of the inner robe, as shown.

STEP 11 Complete the inner robe by applying mauve to the center stripe.

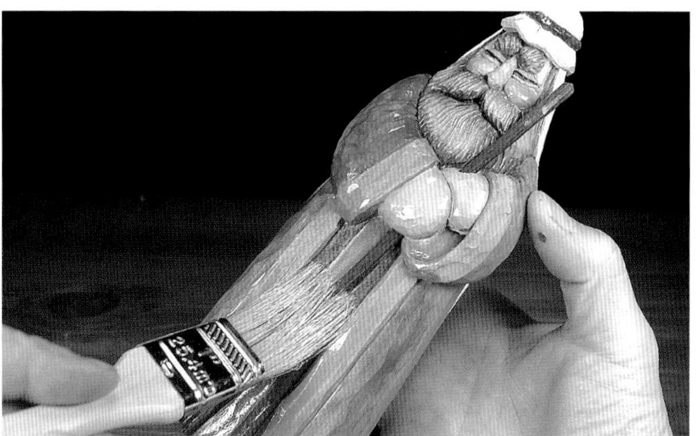

STEP 12 As final touches, deepen the shadowed area of the inner left sleeve with a thin wash of dark blue, and paint in eyelashes on the edge of the closed eyelids with dark brown. Use a very fine detail brush for the lashes. Let the carving dry for at least an hour.

STEP 13 Seal the carving with satin polyurethane. Apply the coat as thinly as you possibly can with a cheap stain brush, scrubbing it into the nooks. Watch the colors pop out as you do this! It will go on shiny, but if you put it on thin, it will dry almost matte. Let the carving dry overnight.

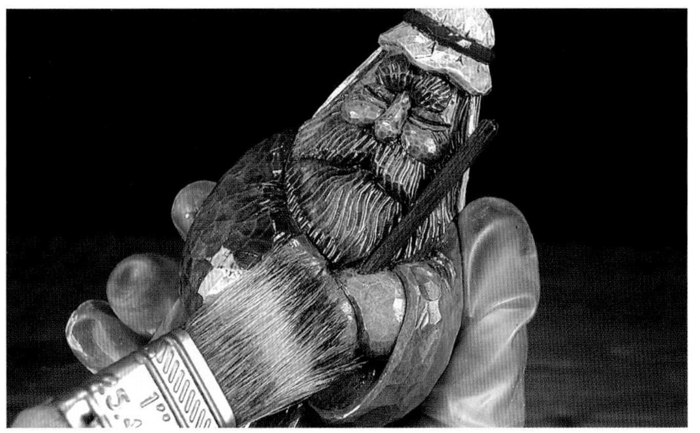

STEP 14 Using the same brush, apply a brown gel wood stain. Slather it on, working it into the nooks.

STEP 15 Immediately wipe off the excess with a clean cotton rag. Let the carving dry overnight before handling it.

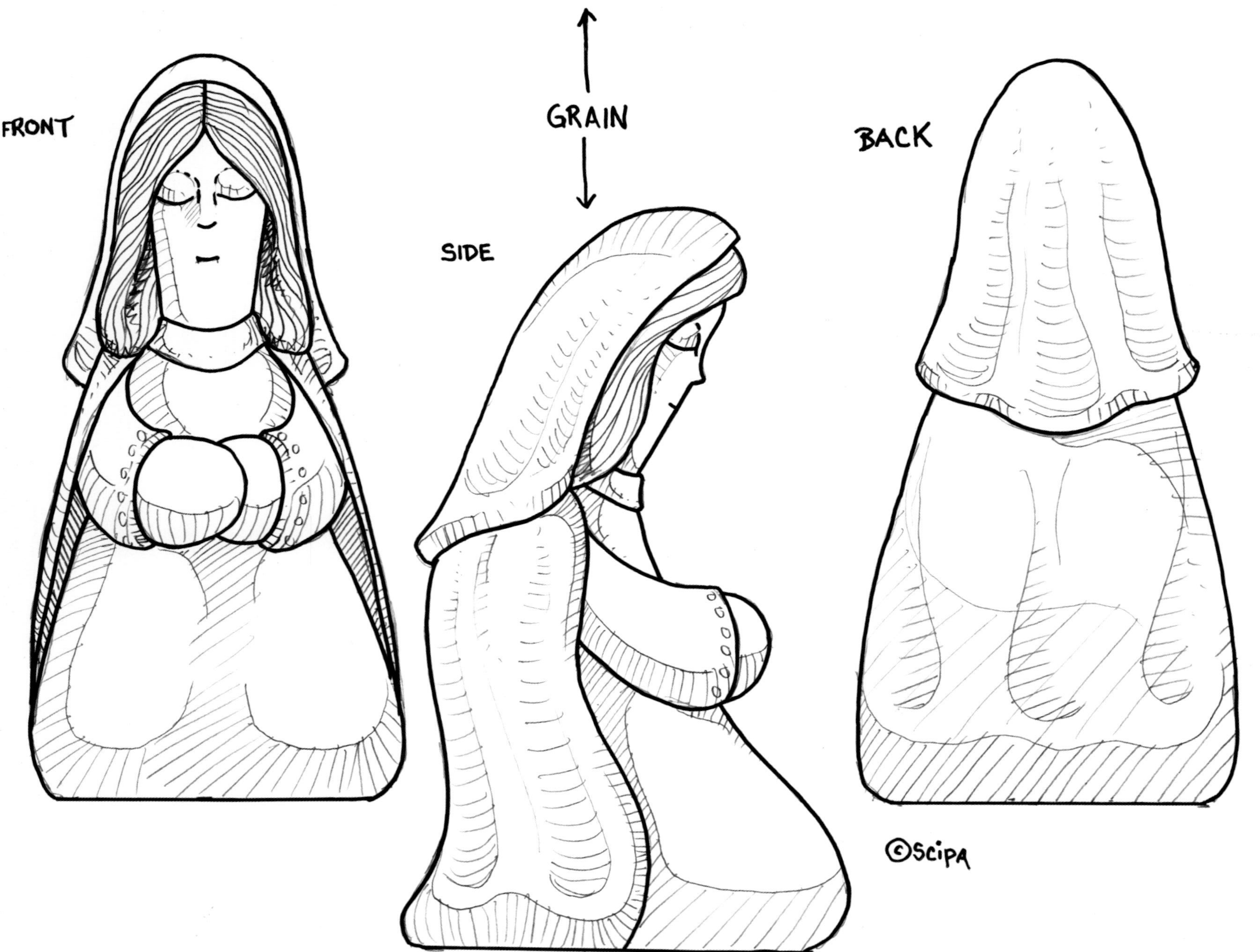
FRONT
GRAIN
SIDE
BACK
©SCIPA

MARY

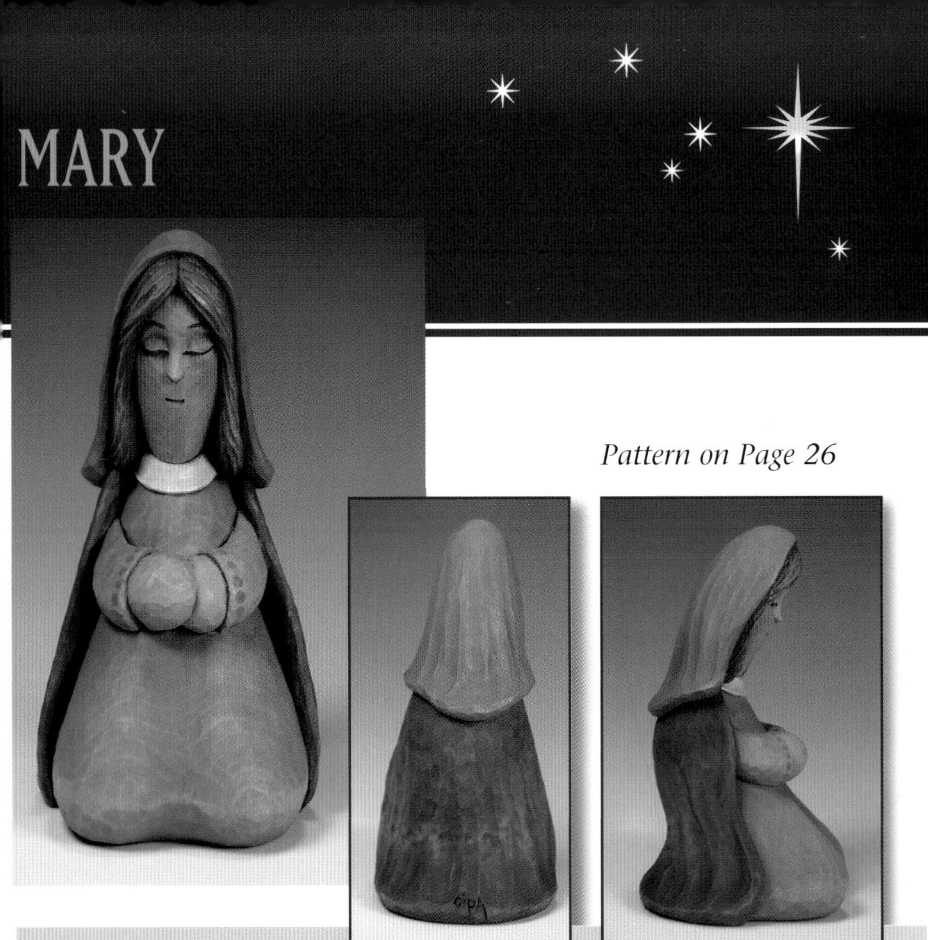

Pattern on Page 26

Materials List: Carving

- Basswood block 3" x 3 1/2" x 6"
- Larger bladed rough-out knife
- Standard carving knife
- Fine detail knife
- #12 3/8" v-tool
- #9 1/2" half-round gouge
- #11 1/8" half-round gouge
- #11 1/16" half-round gouge (veiner)
- 1/4" shallow gouge
- Pencil or fine marker
- Band saw
- Carving glove or thumb tape for protection

Materials List: Painting and Finishing

- 1/2" flat brush for large areas
- 1/4" round brush for smaller areas
- 1/8" round brush
- Very fine detail brush
- Cornflower blue
- Blue-gray
- Light gray
- Light brown
- Dark brown
- Flesh tone
- Bright red
- White
- Fast drying satin polyurethane
- Brown gel wood stain
- Disposable stain brush
- Cotton rag

Mary makes an excellent second demonstration because her body and facial designs make a good template for some of the other carvings in the overall project, such as the kneeling figures and the angels.

The carving techniques implemented in Joseph's lesson also apply here. However, this carving is a bit more difficult because of the kneeling posture of the figure. Mary's body profile is somewhat S-shaped, which presents several changes in grain direction. Be aware of these changes as you carve, especially when carving the face. The bowed head forces you to make all your tapering cuts from the top to the bottom. Be careful when working on the nose in particular; it can easily chip out. The natural tendency is to taper the bridge of the nose from the bottom up. If you forget yourself and do this, it will pop right off (I've learned this the hard way)! If this does happen to you, all is not lost. Simply glue it back on with a touch of instant crazy glue. Once it has dried, you can smooth over the fractured area by going over it with your tools.

If you choose to paint Mary, I have provided a color scheme that matches Joseph's. You can, of course, choose your own. If you choose to apply a natural finish, simply follow the instructions I have provided in Joseph's lesson.

Your block before sawing will need to measure 3"x 3 1/2" x 6".

Carve The Virgin Mary...

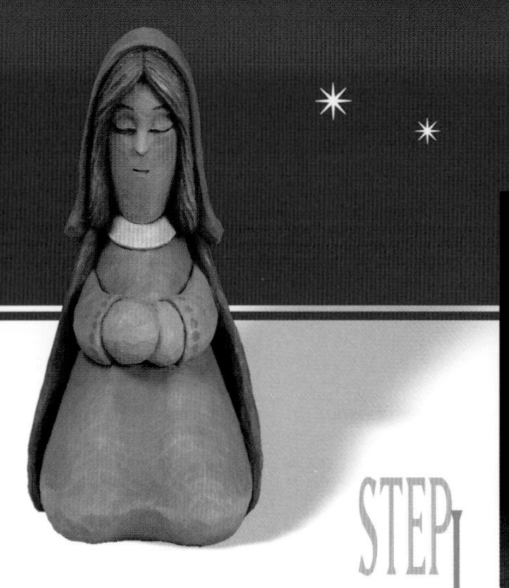

STEP 1

The front view of the band-sawed blank.

STEP 2

The side view. Notice I have band-sawed the hard corners off. When doing this, take very little from the front portion of the head.

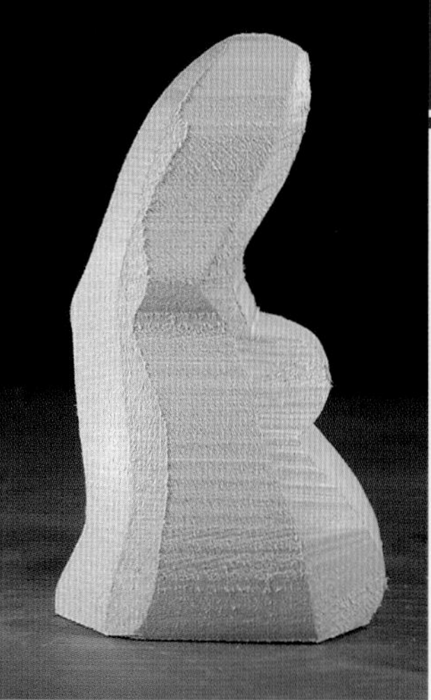

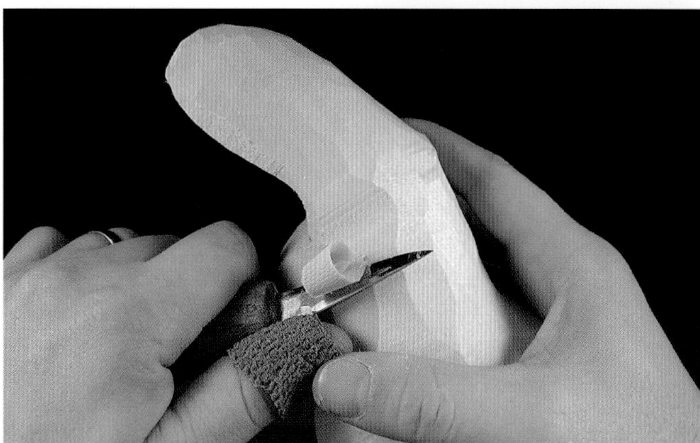

STEP 3

Using your rough-out knife, round out all corners and erase the saw marks. Avoid altering the general shape of the figure too much. Leave the facial area alone for now.

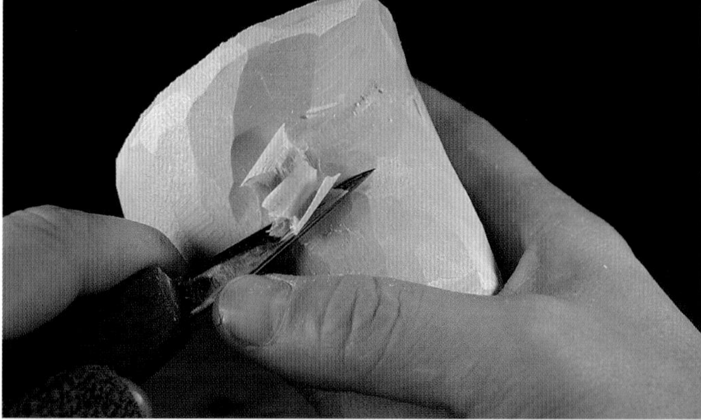

STEP 4

In this roughing-out stage, the grain changes direction often due to the kneeling posture of the figure. Be sure to alternate knife cuts and always follow the grain.

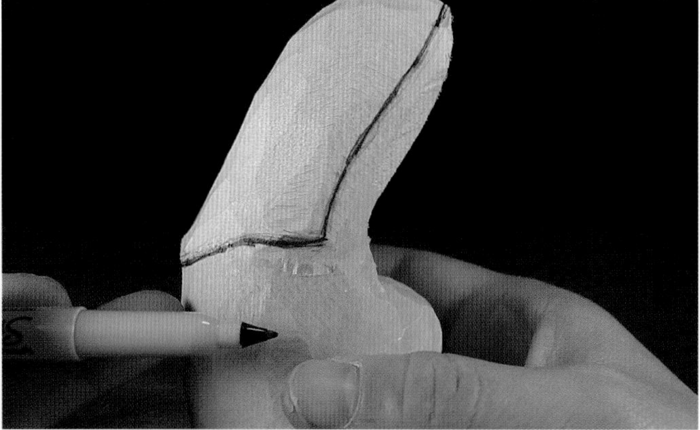

STEP 5

Draw in the veil. Refer to the patterns for correct placement from all views.

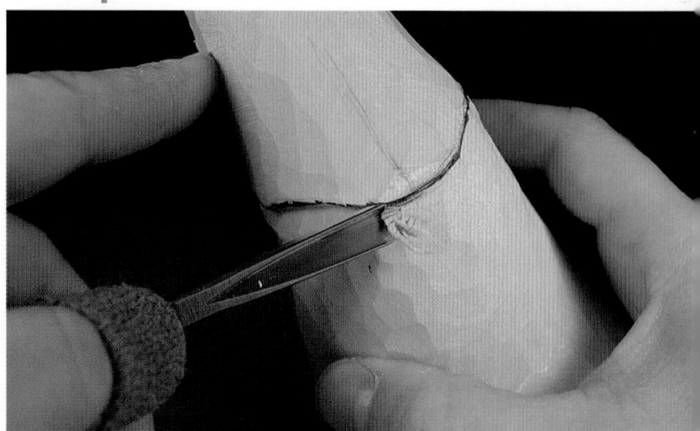

STEP 6

Using the 3/8" v-tool, define the veil by trenching out along the lines. Start in the back. Go about a 1/4" deep.

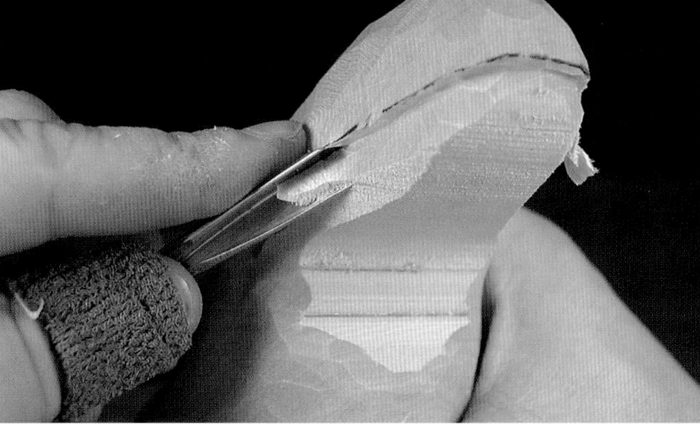

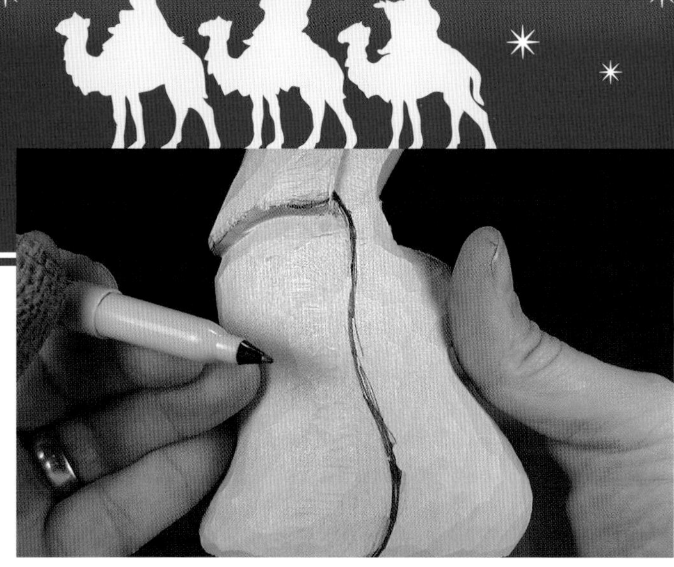

STEP 7 Now do the front, using the v-tool as a plane to shave off excess wood as you go. Don't go as deep in the front.

STEP 8 Draw in the shawl. Refer to the pattern; the line should start just above the bottom corner of the veil, as shown. Draw in both sides.

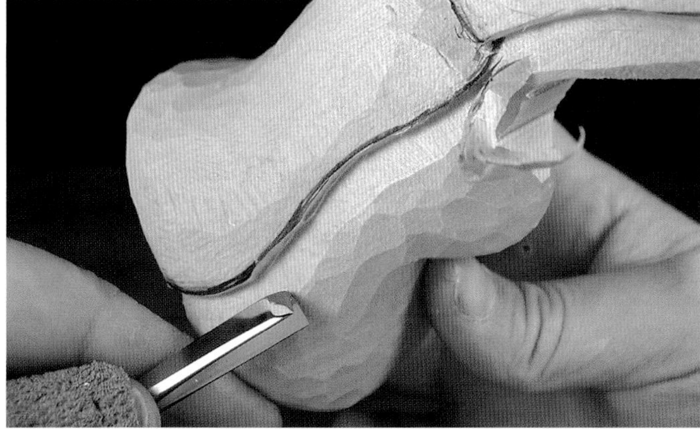

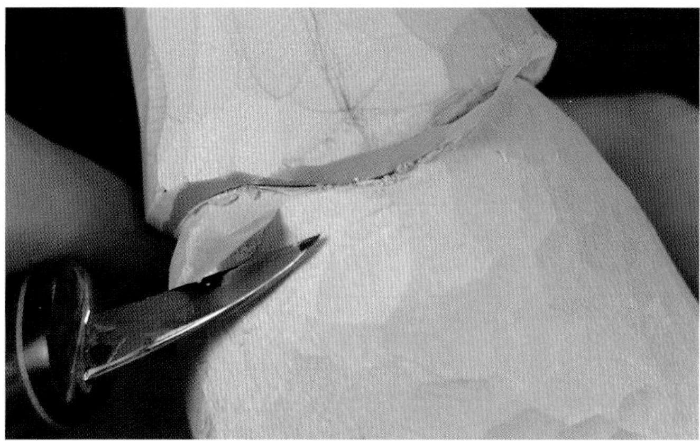

STEP 9 Using the v-tool, trench out the shawl as was done with the veil. Do both sides.

STEP 10 Using a knife, re-trace all v-cuts made thus far with plunging stop cuts. Clean them up by tapering. Smooth out where the back meets the veil...

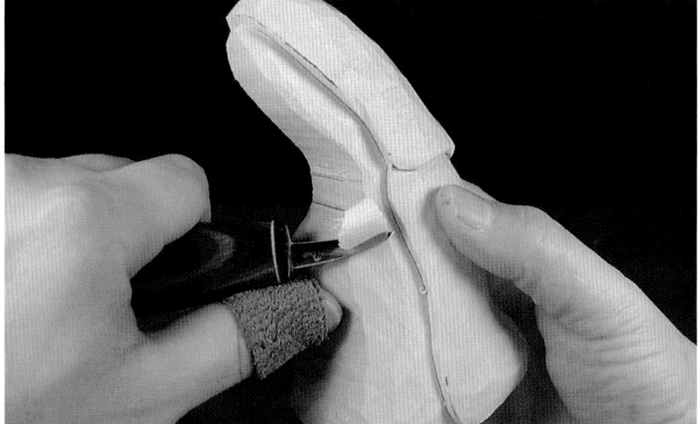

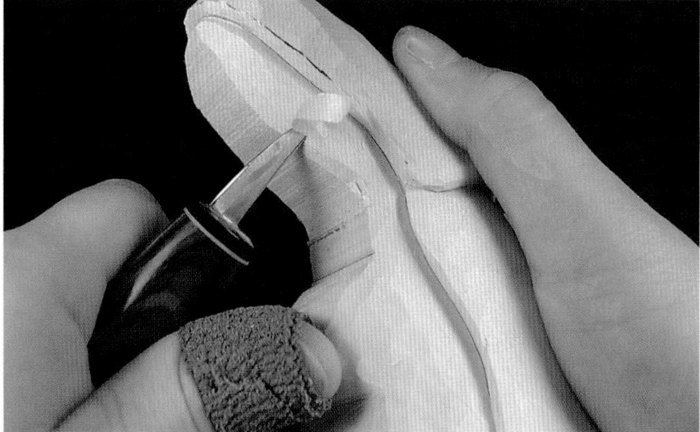

STEP 11 ...and round the front of the body.

STEP 12 Round out the facial area. Notice that the grain is traveling downward because of the bowed head. All cuts must be made from top to bottom.

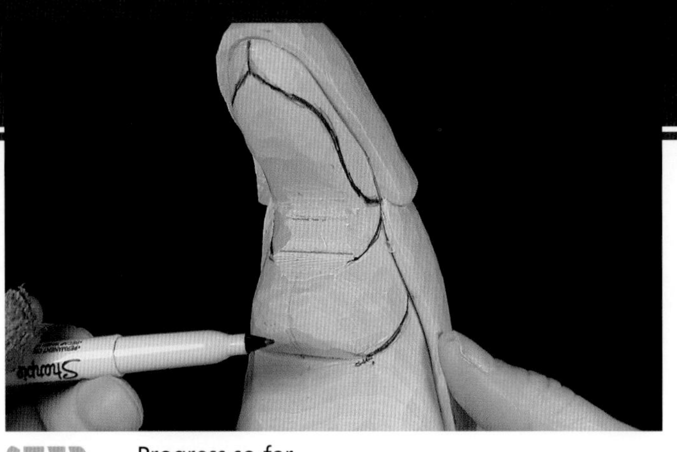

STEP 13 Progress so far.
I have drawn in the arms and the hair.

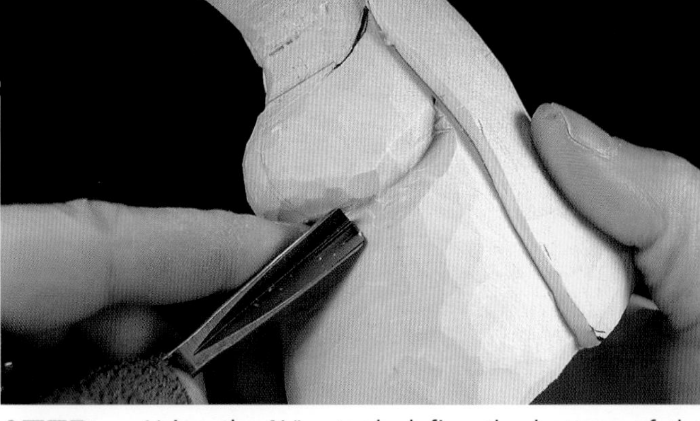

STEP 14 Using the 3/8" v-tool, define the bottom of the arms from the lower body. Do both sides. Don't touch the top of the arms yet.

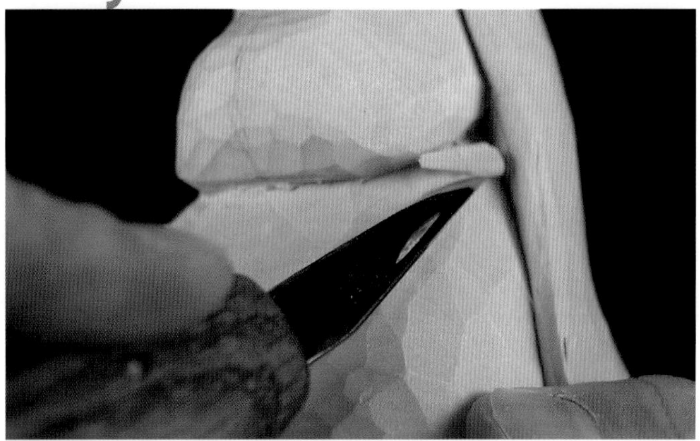

STEP 15 Switching back to the rough-out knife, further define the separation by cleaning up the v-cut and hollowing out under the pits. Make a clear separation between the lap and shawl. Also, taper the lap area up to the arms.

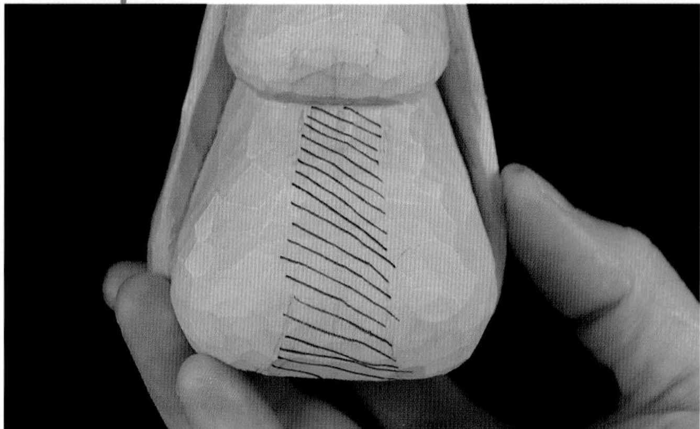

STEP 16 The result. Notice that I have gone fairly deep between the lap and shawl. I have shaded the area to be removed in order to accentuate the valley formed between the legs.

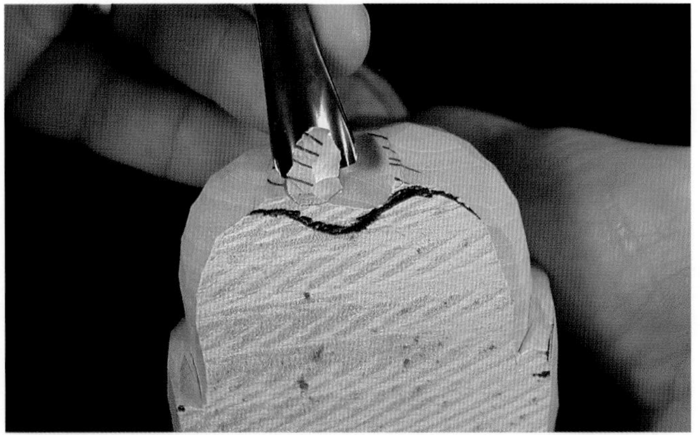

STEP 17 Using a 1/2" half-round gouge, start to hollow out the shallow valley. Begin at the bottom where the knees are. Notice the indent that is forming from the underside.

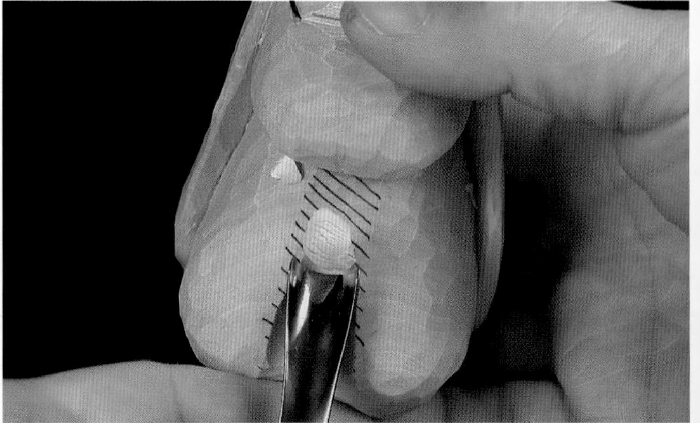

STEP 18 Follow this up to the hands. Keep it shallow; we only want the suggestion of separate legs.

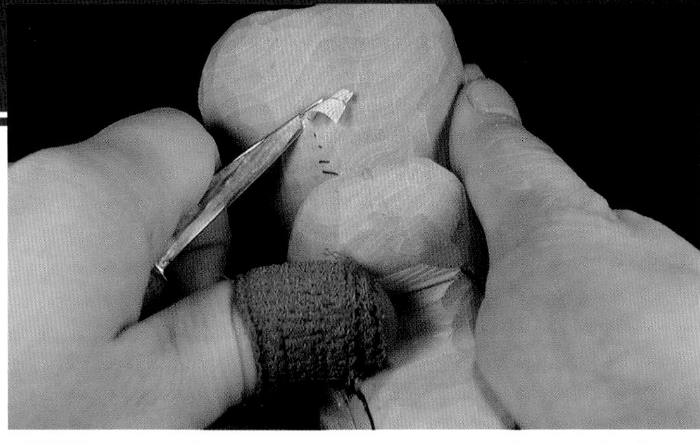

STEP 19 Go back over the hollow with the knife in order to smooth out the gouge marks. Mind the changes in grain direction, especially around the knees!

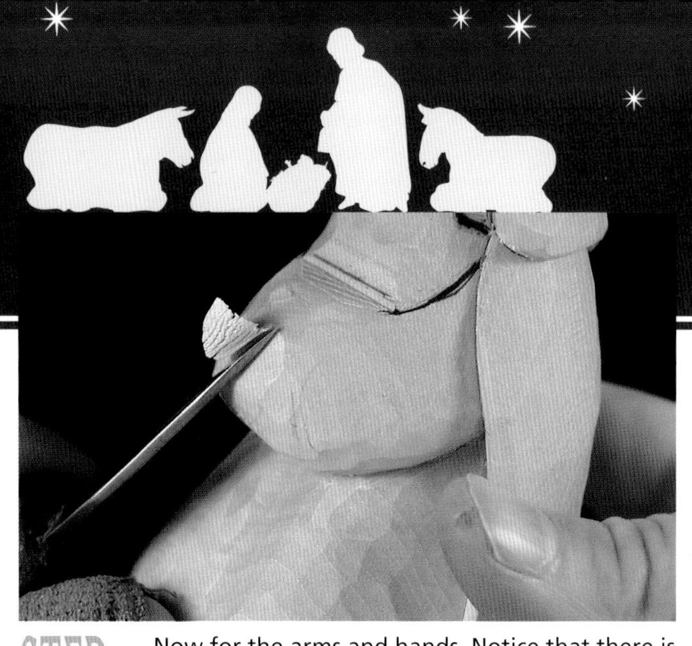

STEP 20 Now for the arms and hands. Notice that there is way too much material here. First, thin out the arm/hand bulge with the rough-out knife. Don't go overboard — you will need some material to work with.

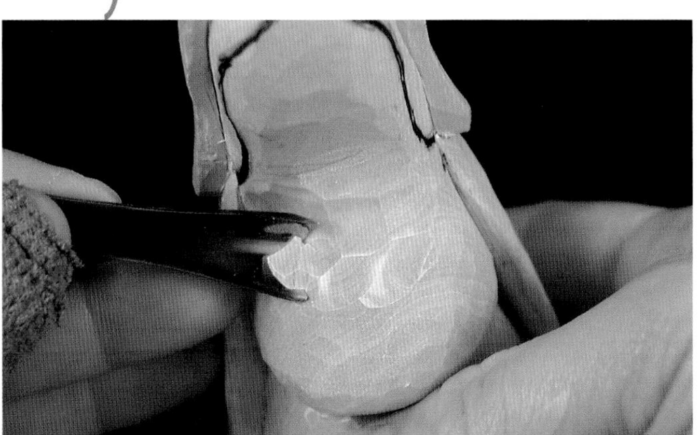

STEP 21 Next, hollow out the chest area a little to help define the shape of the arms. The 1/2" half-round gouge works great here.

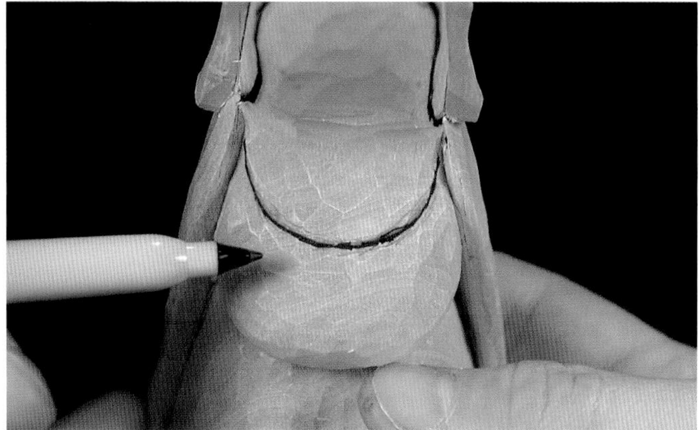

STEP 22 Once you have it at the right proportion (refer to your profile pattern), draw in the division between the arms and chest.

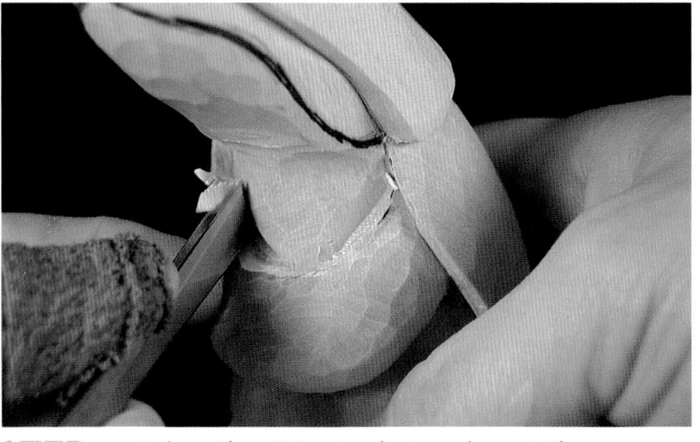

STEP 23 Using the 3/8" v-tool, trench out the separation. This can be a little difficult; it's almost like cutting into end grain. Make sure the v-tool is very sharp!

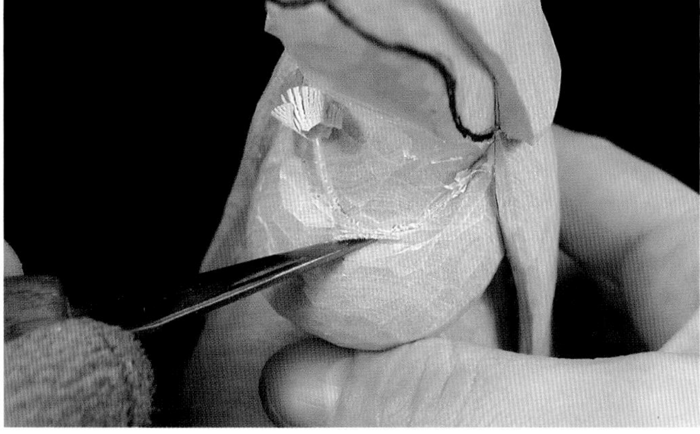

STEP 24 Using the knife, clean up the v-cut and round out the arm/hand area. Taper the chest back a little, just enough to get it out of your way. We'll concentrate on that area later.

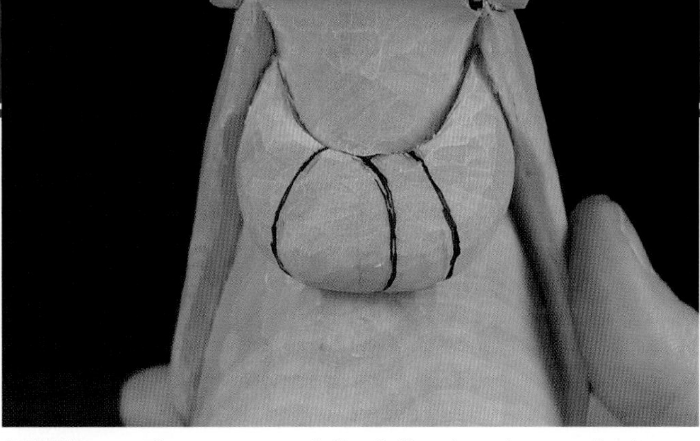

STEP 25 The arms are fully defined and smoothed out. Notice how they seem to disappear into the shawl. I have drawn in the sleeves and hands.

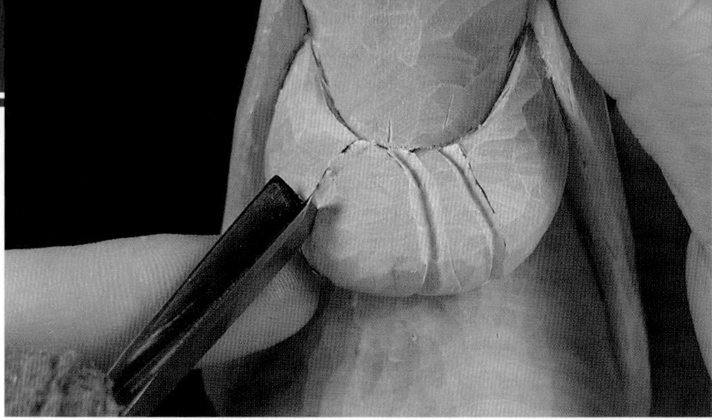

STEP 26 Define the sleeves and hands. I like to use the v-tool first, and then go over it with the standard knife. Notice how her right hand overlaps the left hand.

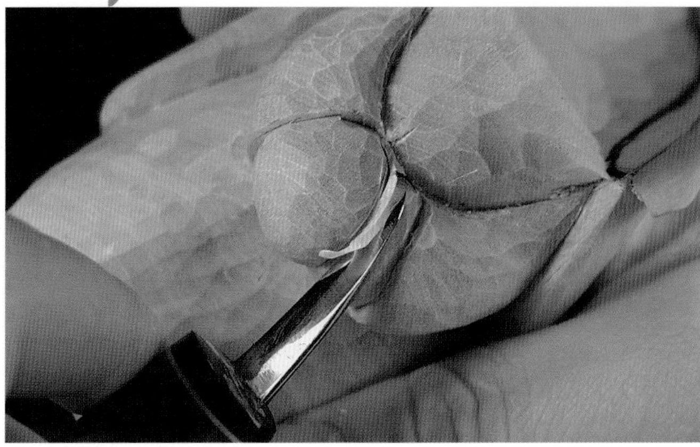

STEP 27 Work the hands into shape with the knife. Round the hand into a mitt-like shape. Her hands will be fingerless for the sake of simplicity, and to keep with the folk art theme.

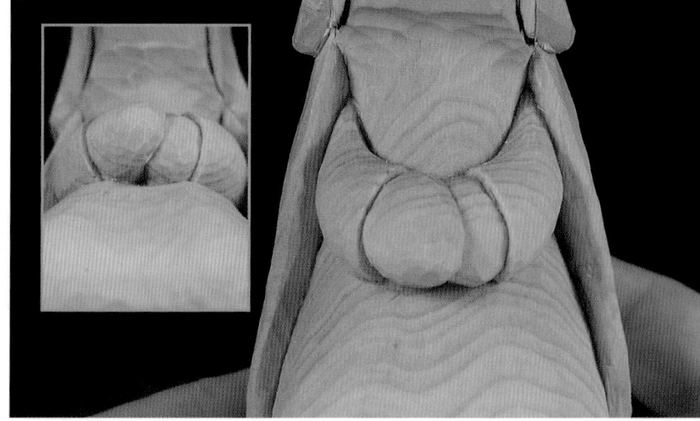

STEP 28 The finished arms and hands. Notice the small chip cut underneath to help simulate the overlap (inset).

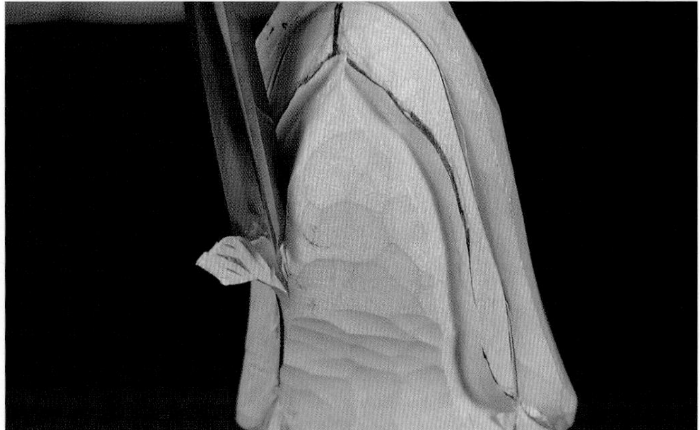

STEP 29 On to the head. First, define the hair we drew in previously by trenching with the $^3/_8$" v-tool. Remember that the grain direction forces us to cut from top to bottom.

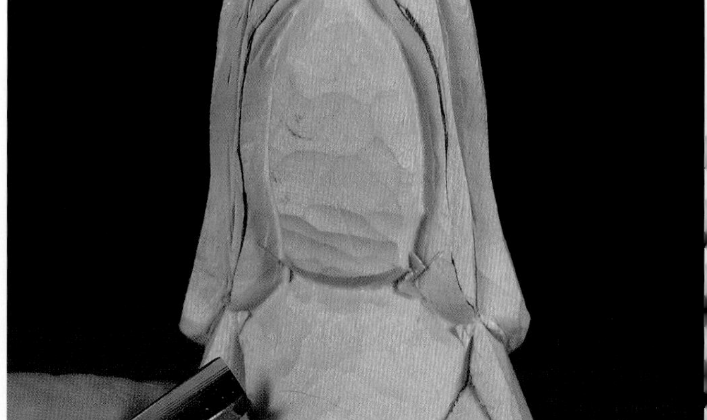

STEP 30 With the v-tool, create a separation between the head and chest, as shown. Refer to the pattern for correct placement.

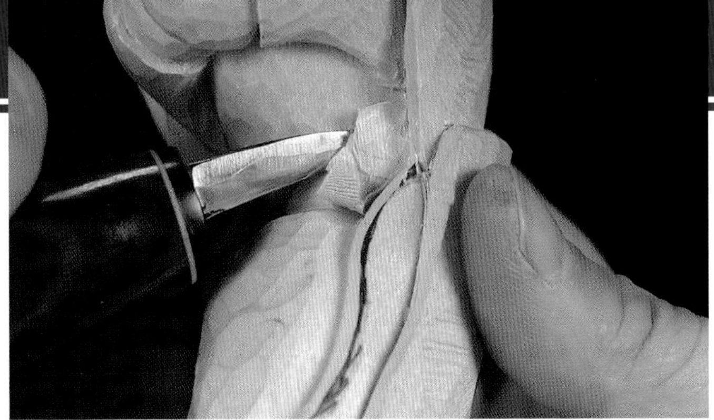

STEP 31 Using the knife, clean up the chest/neckline area. This is a complex area because the face, hair, neckline, and shawl all intersect here. Taper the chest up to the neckline.

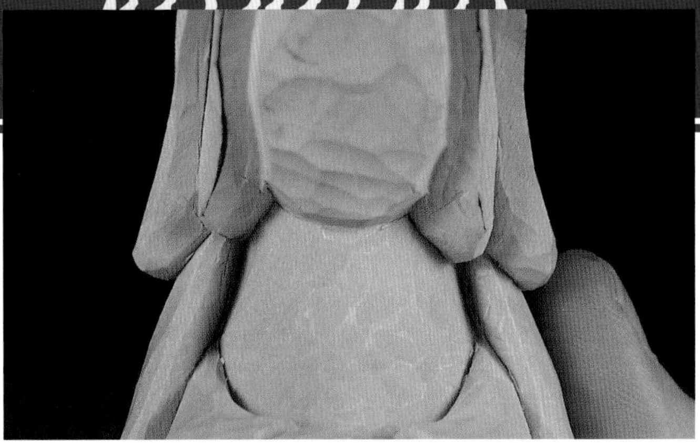

STEP 32 Progress so far. It should look something like this. I have gone deep between the shoulders and the shawl. The shawl seems to disappear under the veil, with the hair hanging over both. The neckline is crisply defined.

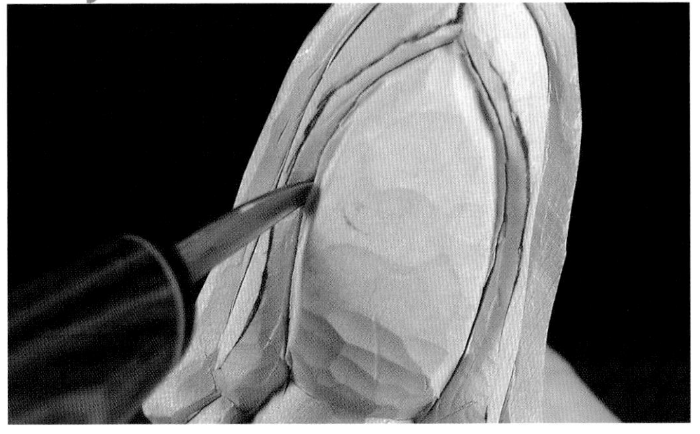

STEP 33 To shape the face, plunge the knife straight into the v-groove between the face and hair. Don't angle the knifepoint toward the face. Try to get it as deep as you can on the first pass in order to keep the cut clean.

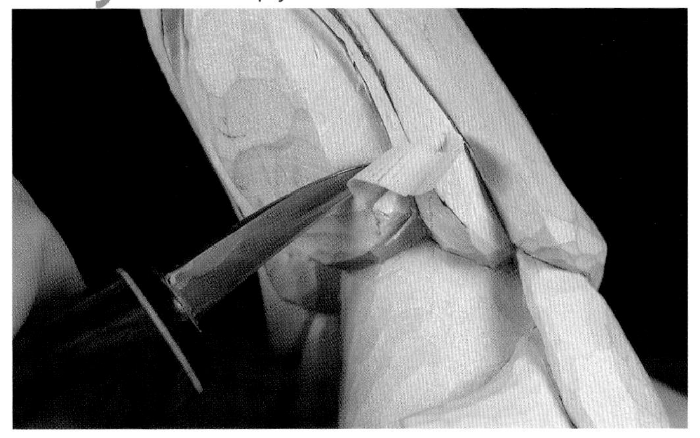

STEP 34 Begin to pare away small amounts of wood on both sides of the cuts to separate the face from the hair. Avoid taking too much from the very front of the face at this point.

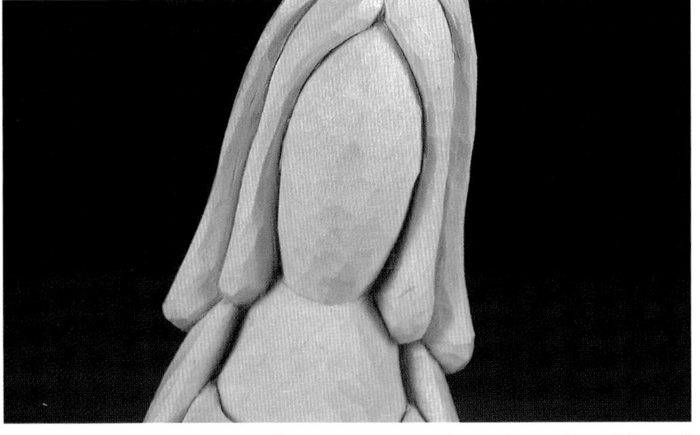

STEP 35 Progress so far. I have cut deep into the sides of the face, maintaining the neckline as I go. I have parted her hair and rounded the hanging locks. I have also shaped the face like an egg, all with the knife.

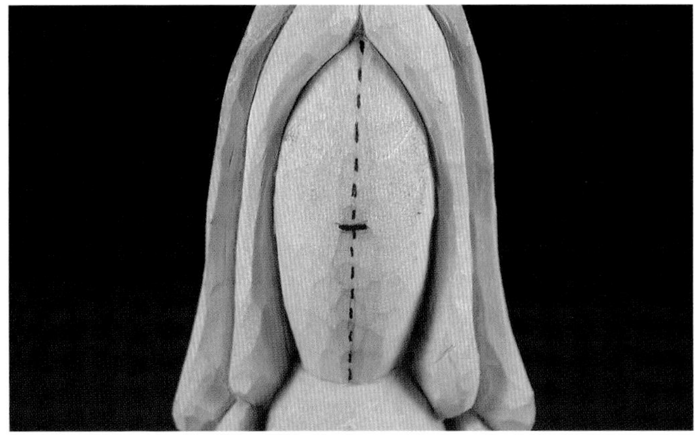

STEP 36 Find the center of the face and make a mark halfway down, as shown. This facial design, with a button nose and closed, reverent eyes, is stylized and meant to be simple, in the folk art style.

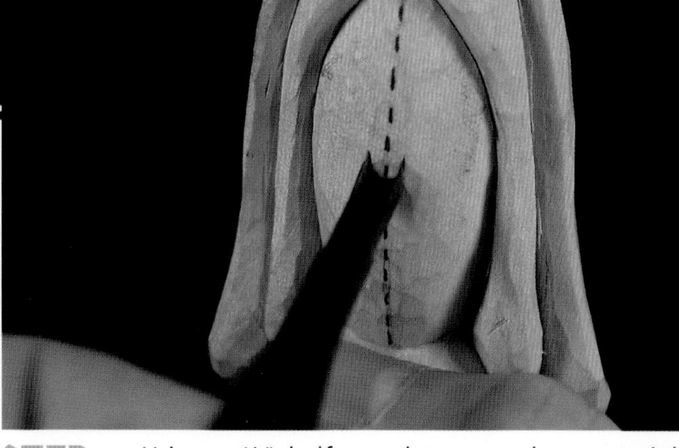

STEP 37 Using a $^1/_8$" half-round gouge, plunge straight into the face. Make sure the bottom of the gouge is placed just above the halfway mark.

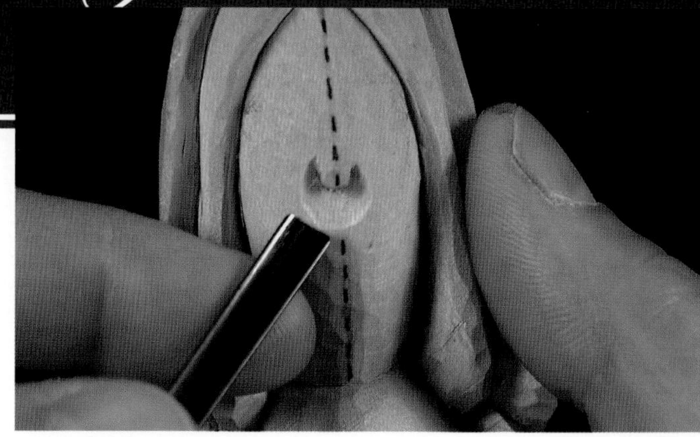

STEP 38 Using a $^1/_4$" shallow gouge, hollow out a pocket below the plunge cut. Be careful not to chip out the nose!

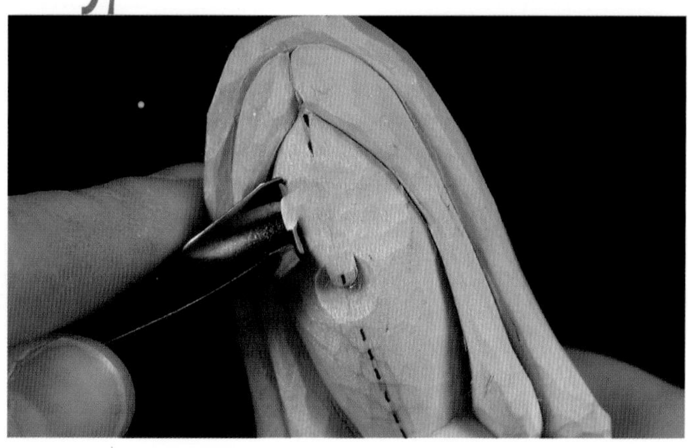

STEP 39 Using the $^1/_2$" half-round gouge, slightly scallop out the wood above the nose to create a sloping bridge. Take small bites at a time, and continue the slope up to the hairline. Because of the grain direction, a gouge used cross-grain works better than a knife.

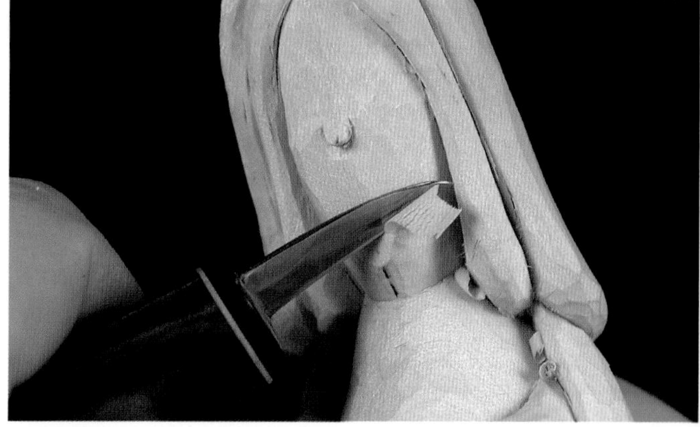

STEP 40 Using the knife, remove wood from the sides and bottom of the face to erase the hollow under the nose. This action brings out the button nose, and makes it the most prominent point on the face. Follow through down to the neckline.

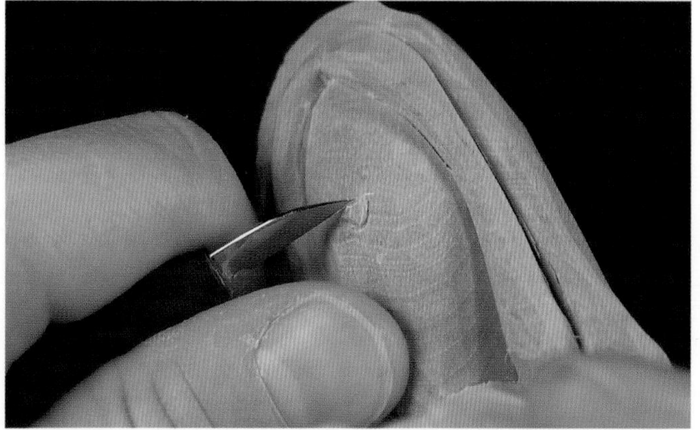

STEP 41 Round off the hard edge of the nose a bit to give it an upturned look. I have switched to a fine detail knife for this step.

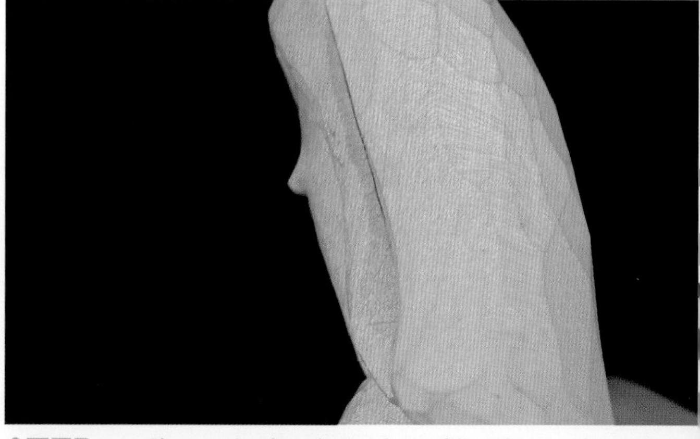

STEP 42 Shown is the desired profile. If you don't have this, repeat the last three steps until you get it right. Although it seems simple enough, the grain direction can make it tricky. Take your time; these steps are crucial for the proper expression.

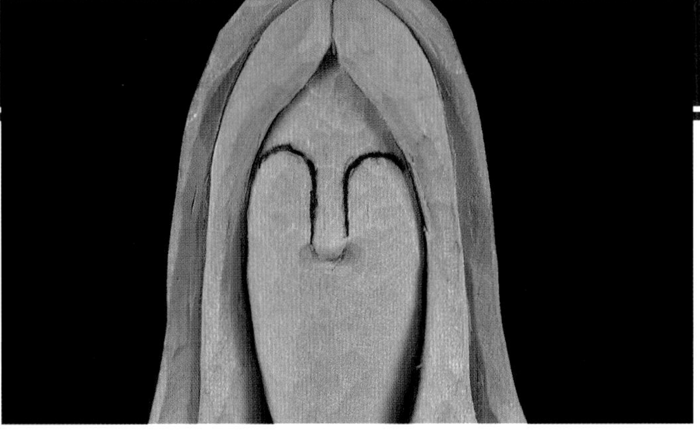

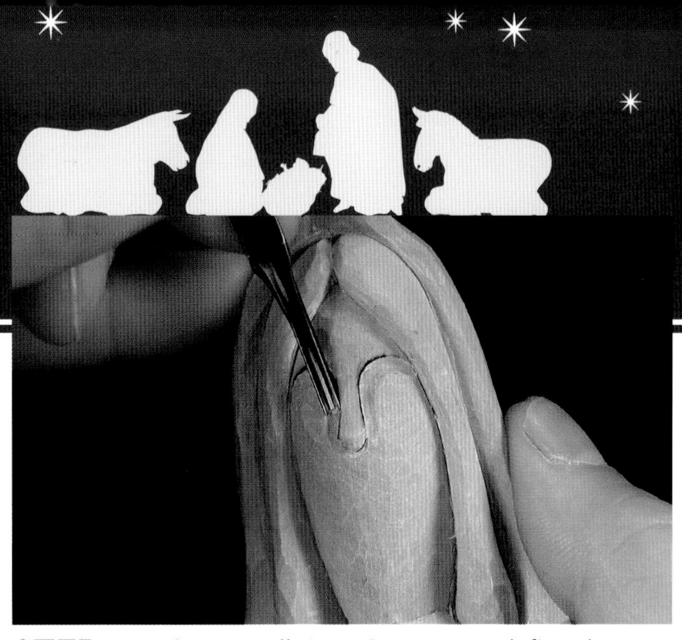

STEP 43 Draw in guidelines for the hollows of the eyes as shown.

STEP 44 Using a small 1/16" veiner gouge, define the nose and the brow line. Because of the grain direction, you may have to start at the top of the nose, do the arch, and go back to do the nose line from top to bottom.

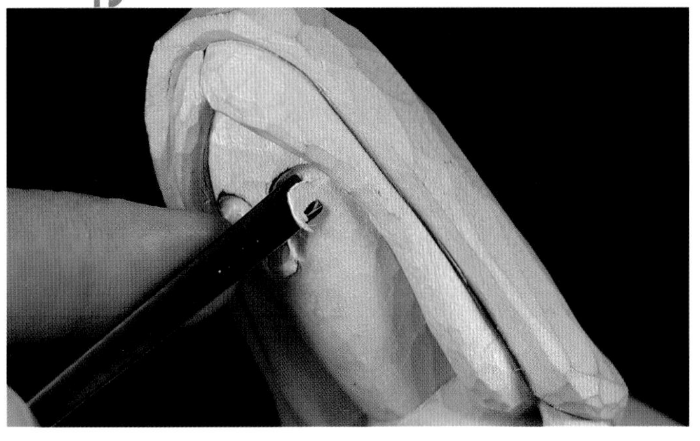

STEP 45 Using the 1/4" shallow gouge, hollow the sockets slightly. Do not create holes or pits; all we want to do is to soften the veiner trenches. Round off the nose bridge and brow line just a bit.

STEP 46 The result. Draw in the closed eyelids as shown.

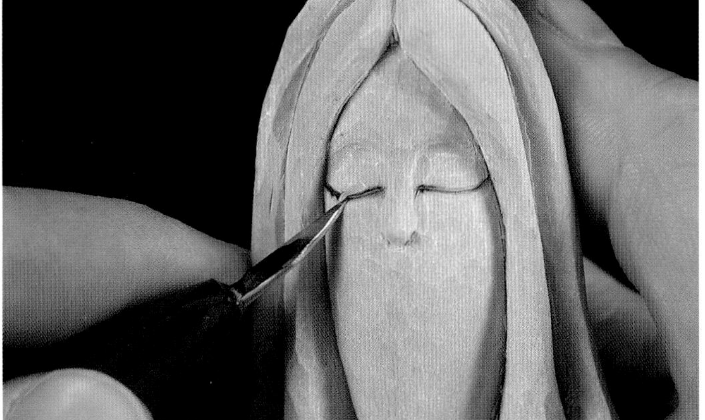

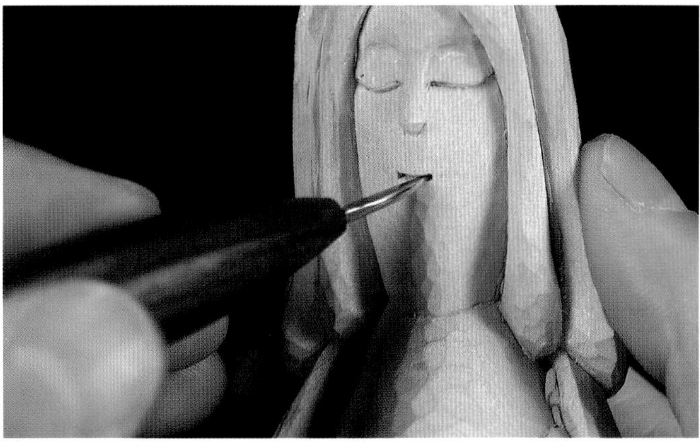

STEP 47 Using the fine detail knife, make a stop cut and remove a shallow slice of wood to define the eyelid. Do both eyes. After that, taper the cheeks a little under the lids. This completes the eyes and nose.

STEP 48 For the mouth, smooth out the area (if it is not already). Create the mouth with a stop cut in the same fashion as the eyelids. To open the mouth a little, plunge the tip of the knife into each corner with the spine of the blade facing outward. Wiggle the knife a bit, compressing the wood fibers.

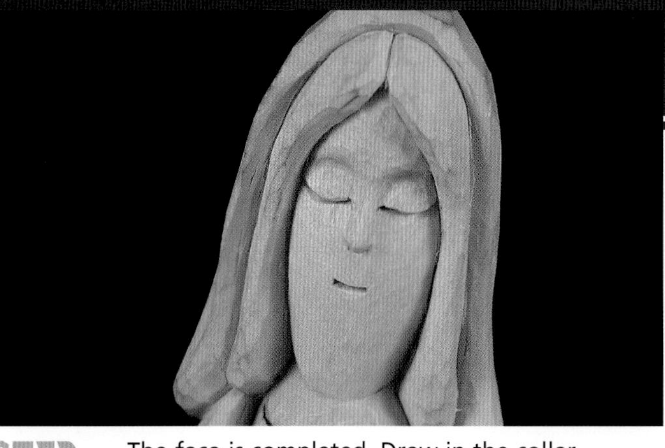

STEP 49 The face is completed. Draw in the collar.

STEP 50 Use the detail knife to define the collar by applying stop and taper cuts.

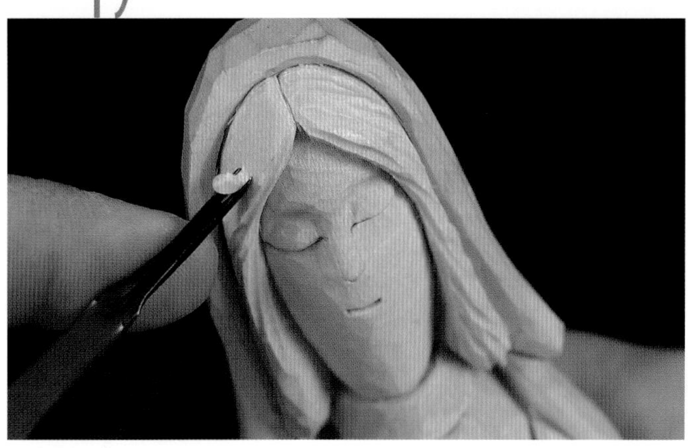

STEP 51 Using the $^1/_{16}$" veiner gouge, create texture in her hair. Try to make it flow down from the part, overlapping and intersecting.

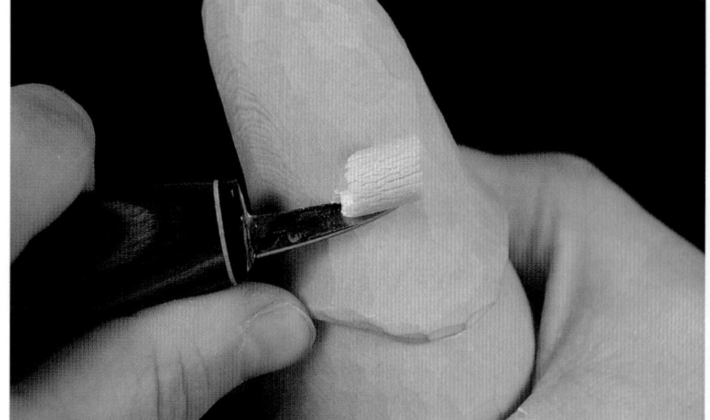

STEP 52 After the hair is complete, you will probably need to thin out the veil around the face, and give it more of a concave slope in the back towards the bottom. Use the knife.

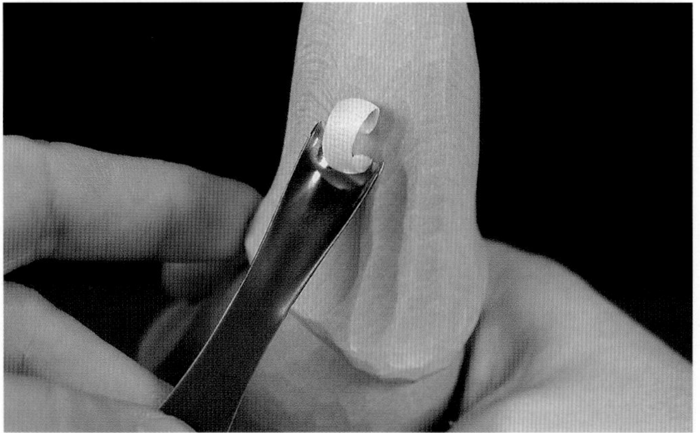

STEP 53 Once you have the veil shaped the way you want, use the $^1/_2$" half-round gouge to create some draping texture. Run shallow grooves from the bottom up, as shown.

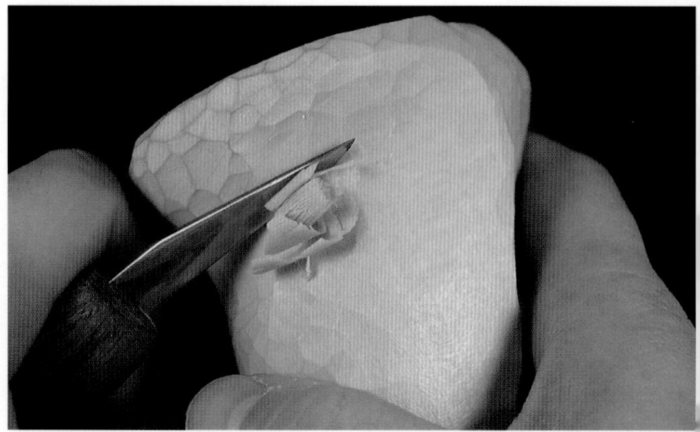

STEP 54 You will also want to give the shawl a final going over. I have thinned out the shoulders and deepened the seat area. Use the knife and be aware of the changing grain direction.

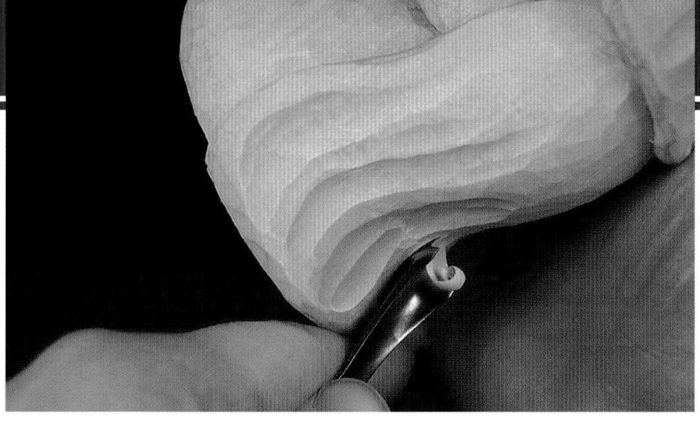

STEP 55 As with the veil, add some draping texture with the 1/2" half-round gouge.

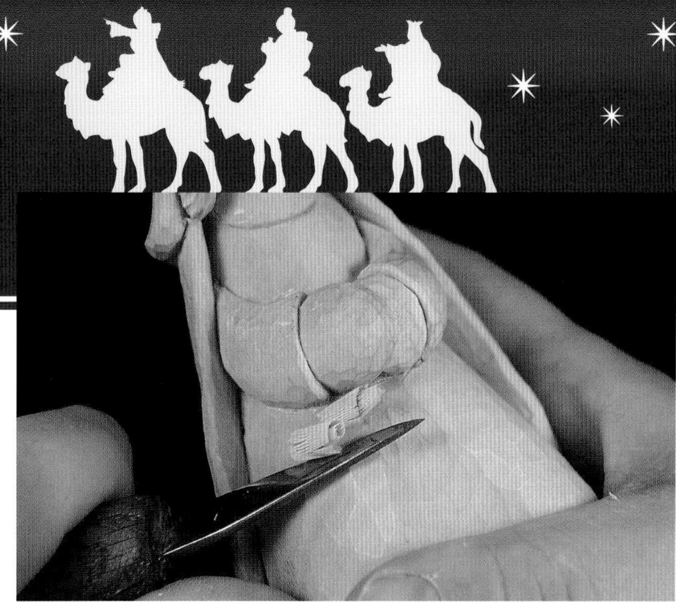

STEP 56 The carving is complete; however, because of the unusual shape of this carving, you may want to go back and fine-tune some areas. I have decided that the lap needs to be tapered more.

STEP 57 Ready for painting!

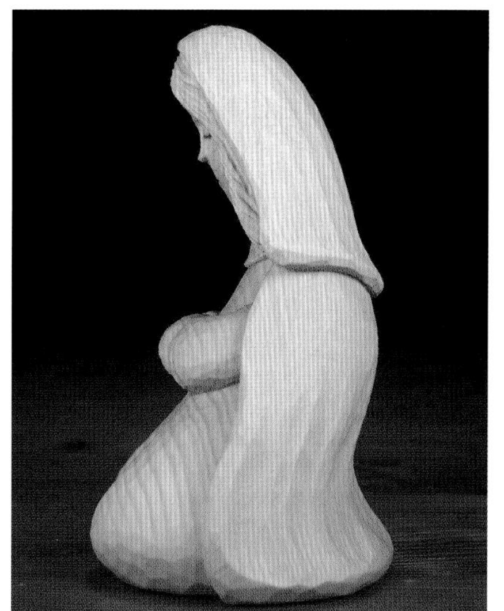

STEP 58 A side view.

Painting Mary

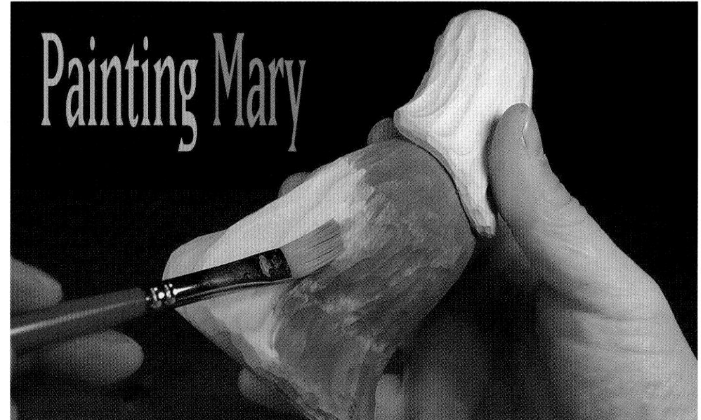

STEP 1 Before painting, lightly clean your carving as you did with Joseph. Once it has dried, apply cornflower blue to Mary's shawl. Use the large brush, with a smaller one for the inner folds.

STEP 2 Paint the veil blue-gray, using the larger brush. Use the smaller one to get around her face.

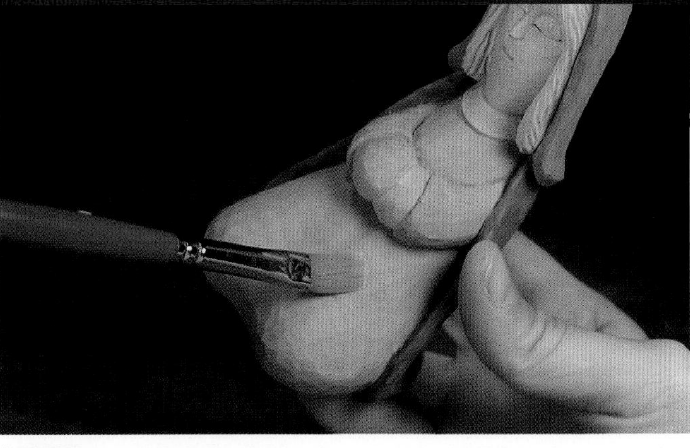

STEP 3 Using both the large and small brush, paint the robe light gray.

STEP 4 Create lowlights in the robe by applying a thin wash of blue-gray in the deep areas and between the legs. Be sure to keep it subtle and blend it in. Use the small round brush.

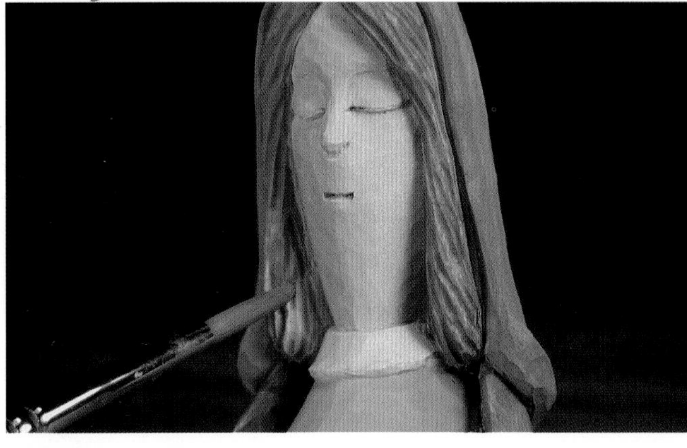

STEP 5 Using the small round brush, apply light brown to the hair. Be careful not to touch the face. If you do, you can erase the mark with your detail knife.

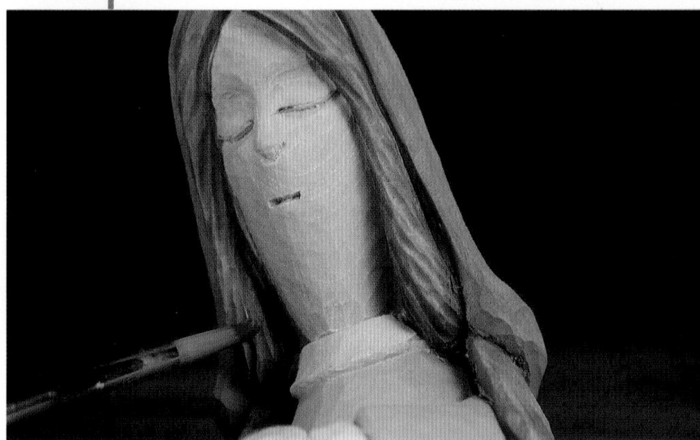

STEP 6 Create lowlights to the hair by applying a thin wash of dark brown to the areas near the face and the edges of the veil. Use the small round brush.

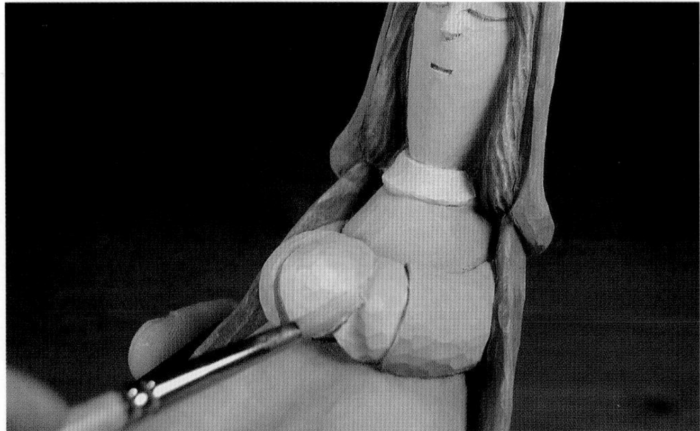

STEP 7 Using the small round brush, apply flesh tone to the face and hands.

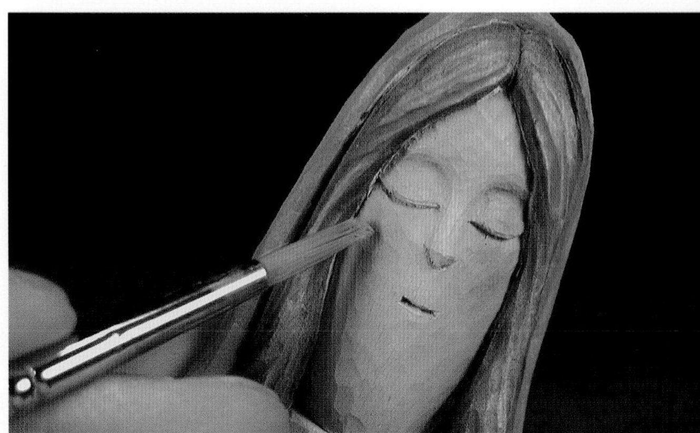

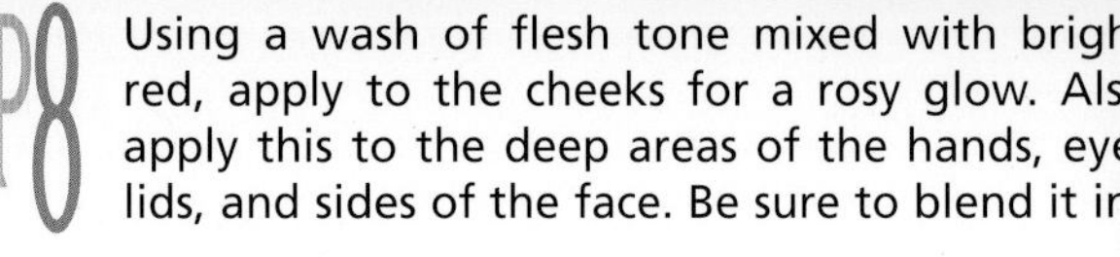

STEP 8 Using a wash of flesh tone mixed with bright red, apply to the cheeks for a rosy glow. Also apply this to the deep areas of the hands, eyelids, and sides of the face. Be sure to blend it in!

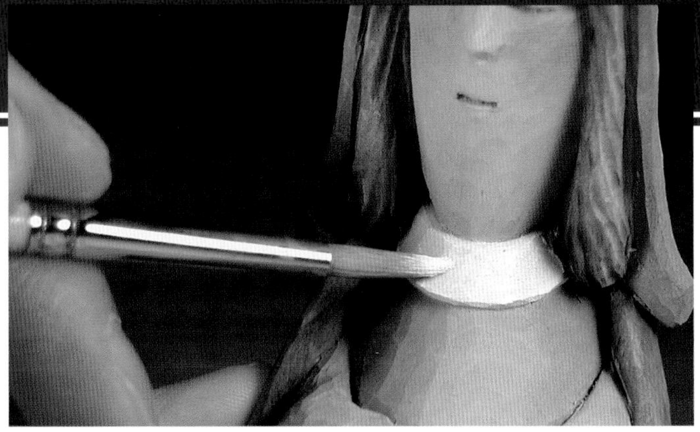

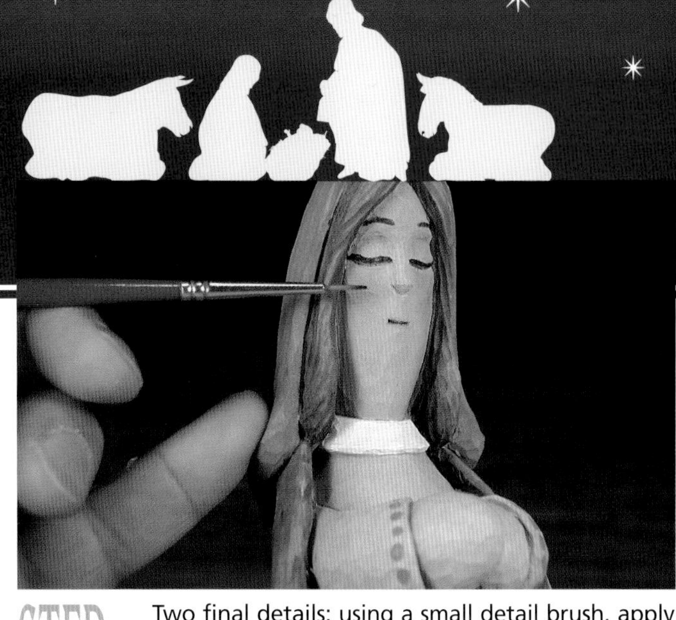

STEP 9 Apply white to the collar.

STEP 10 Two final details: using a small detail brush, apply decorative dots along the cuffs with blue-gray. Also, paint in eyelashes on the ridge of the closed eyelids and thin eyebrows, as shown. Use dark brown. Let the carving dry for at least an hour.

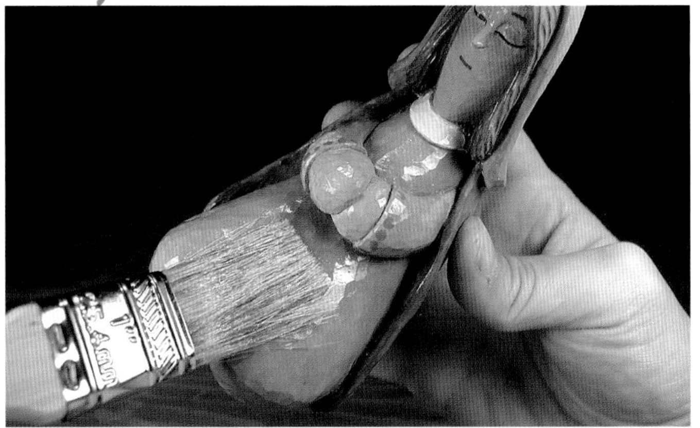

STEP 11 Seal the carving with satin polyurethane. Using a stain brush, apply the sealer coat as thinly as possible, scrubbing into the nooks. This will seal the carving for the antique process.

STEP 12 Apply the antique gel wood stain, slathering it on so it gets into the crevices.

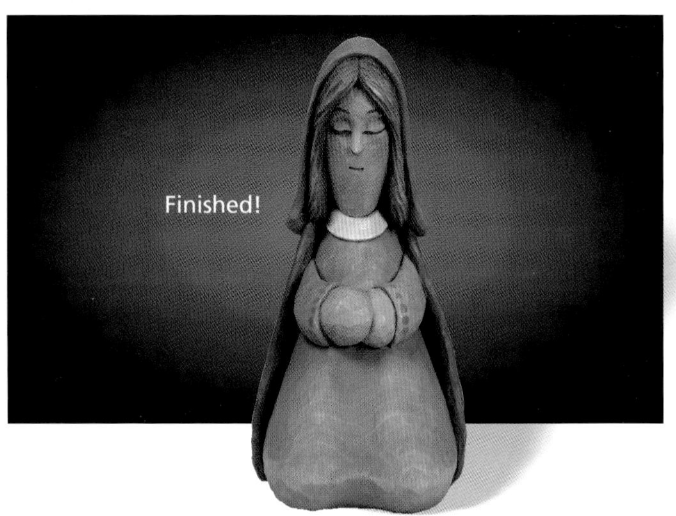

Finished!

STEP 13 Immediately wipe away the excess with a cotton cloth. Let the carving dry overnight before handling it.

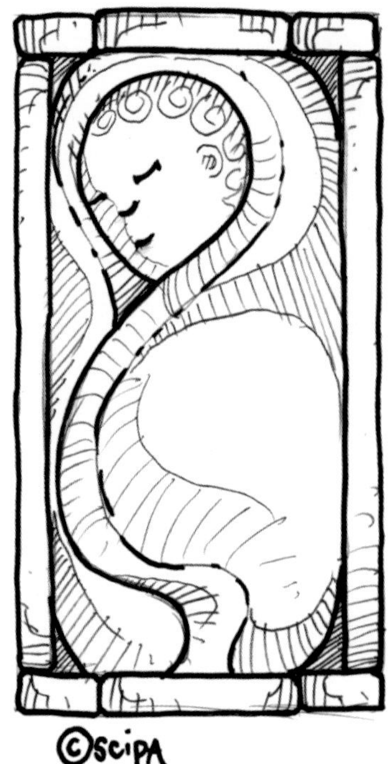

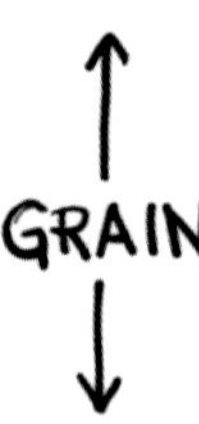

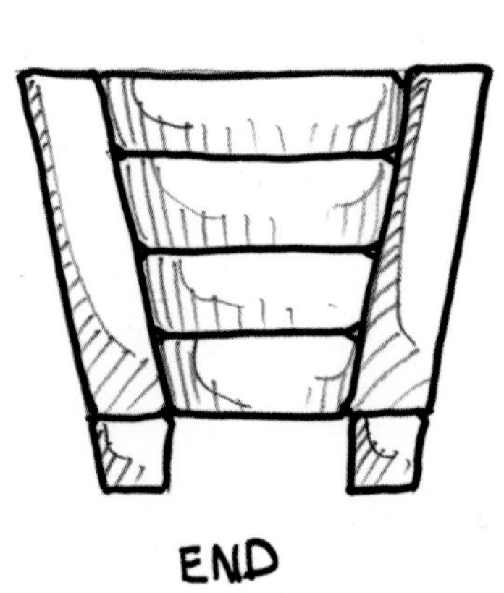

END

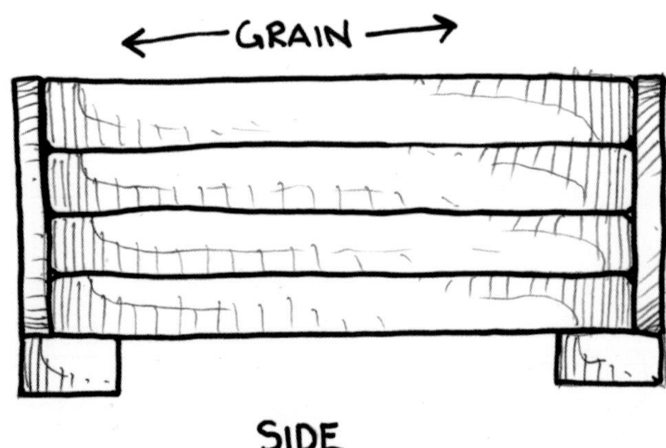

SIDE

THE HOLY CHILD

Pattern on Page 40

This project is fairly simple to complete, and shouldn't take you much time. The Holy Child portion of the carving is a good example of relief work, that is, creating the illusion of depth without really going that deep at all.

The Child's face has very minimal features, yet an expression of peaceful contentment is obvious. This is not hard at all to accomplish when the facial elements are correctly placed. Sometimes simplicity says much more than detail would. How ironic it is that the most simplistic piece in the whole Nativity project is the most important conceptually!

When band-sawing out the blank, be sure to cut out the voids that define the manger's feet before cutting the angled sides. The easiest way to define the angles is to saw the blank while standing it on end. Then follow the end view pattern. If you don't want to deal with this, simply eliminate the feet and go with a flat bottom.

Your block before sawing will need to measure 1 1/4" x 1 1/4" x 3 1/4".

Materials List: Carving

Basswood block 1 1/4" x 1 1/4" x 3 1/4"
Standard carving knife
Fine detail knife
#12 3/8" v-tool
#12 1/8" v-tool
#11 1/4" half-round gouge
Very small veiner gouge
1/8" shallow gouge
1/4" shallow gouge
1/2" fishtail gouge
Pencil or fine marker
Band saw
Carving glove or thumb tape for protection

Materials List: Painting and Finishing

1/2" flat brush for large areas
1/4" round brush for smaller areas
1/8" round brush
Raw sienna
Antique white
Corn yellow
Flesh tone
Bright red
Medium gray
Fast drying satin polyurethane
Brown gel wood stain
Disposable stain brush
Cotton rag

Carve The Holy Child...

STEP 1

The band-sawed blank. If you don't want to bother with the feet, simply eliminate them.

STEP 2

The first thing to do is the outside of the manger. Using a ½" fishtail gouge, skim the outer surfaces to erase the saw marks. You could use a knife, but I prefer the gouge; it creates more texture. Do the sides first.

STEP 3

Do the ends next. The gouge definitely works better on the end-grain than a knife would.

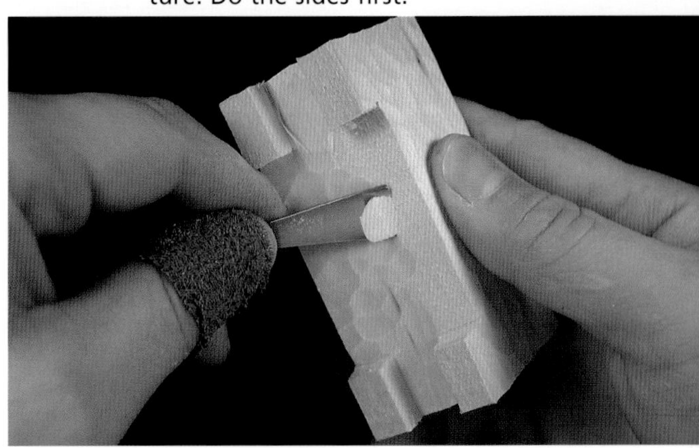

STEP 4

Do the bottom. Don't worry about the feet; we'll do those with a knife.

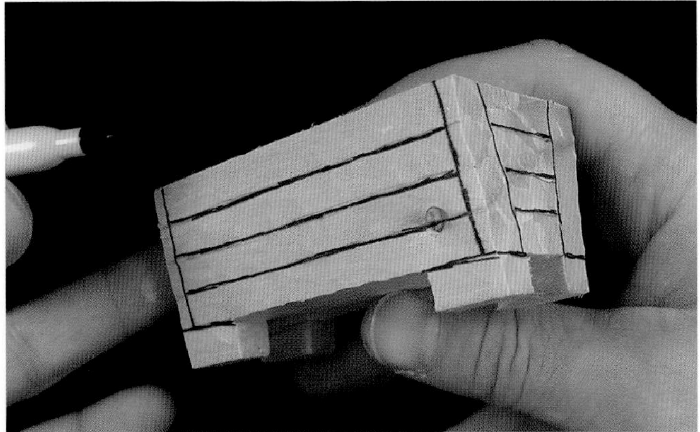

STEP 5

Referring to the pattern, draw in the planks as shown.

STEP 6

Using a small ⅛" v-tool, define each plank by retracing along the lines.

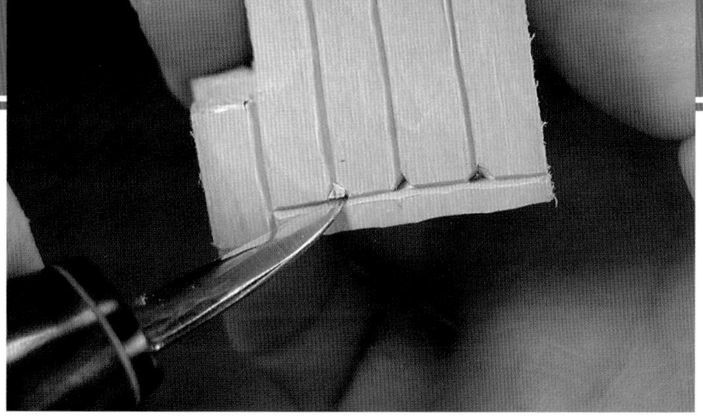

STEP 7 Using a knife, make tiny chip cuts at each intersecting line, as shown. This helps to make the planks more three-dimensional and rustic looking. While you have the knife in hand, bevel all corners and shape the feet.

STEP 8 The outer manger is complete.

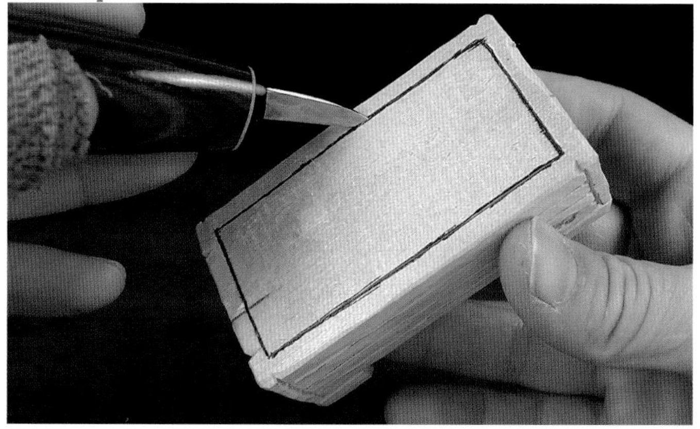

STEP 9 Now for the baby. The Holy Child will be more or less a deep relief carving, carved into the top surface of the manger. Draw in a rectangle as shown, and plunge cut deeply along these lines with your knife. Be sure to follow the angle of the outer sides!

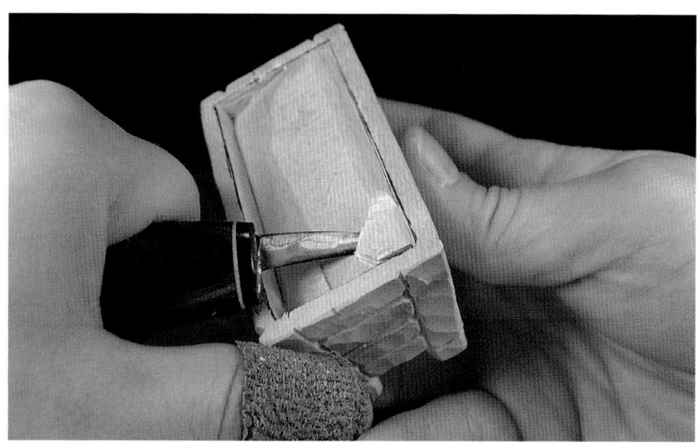

STEP 10 Using the knife, carve away the inner edges as shown. The idea is to form a kind of mound. Don't go any deeper than 3/8" or so on the edges.

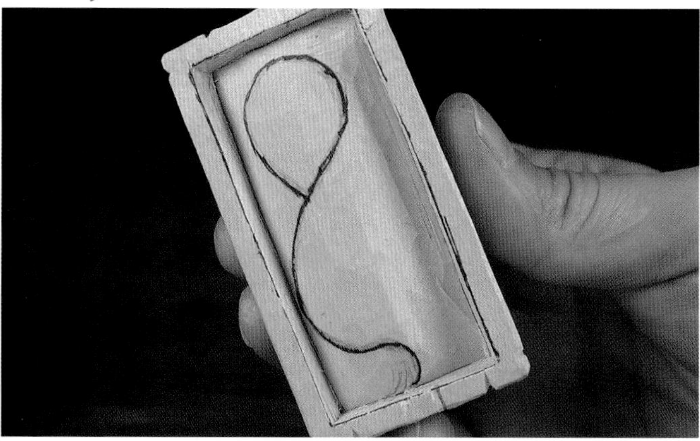

STEP 11 Notice the mound effect. Draw in the main blanket line. Refer to the pattern for this; the placement is critical.

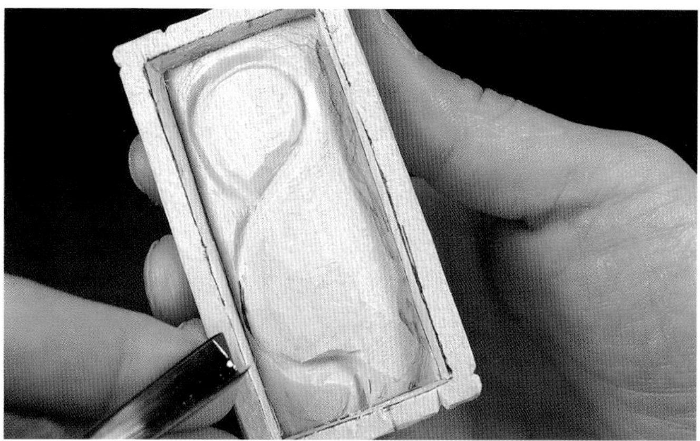

STEP 12 Using a 3/8" v-tool, follow the blanket line to create a groove like the one shown. Try to have the v-groove centered where the line was.

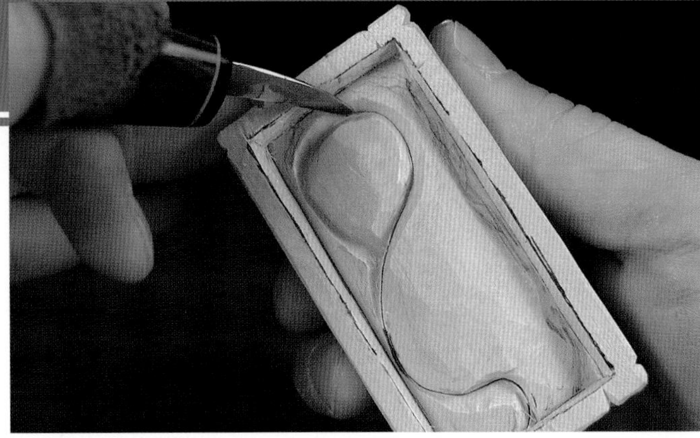

STEP 13 Using the knife, further define the v-groove first by plunge cutting...

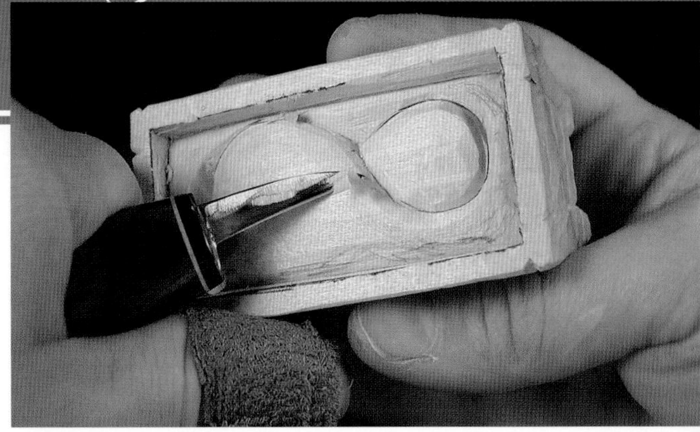

STEP 14 ...and second by smoothing out the groove, making it more fluid. Study the photo of the finished piece. The left side of the blanket should appear to be overlapped by the larger right side.

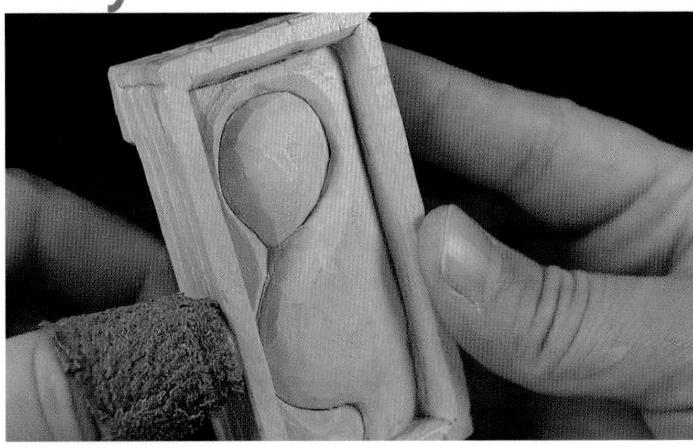

STEP 15 Progress so far. Notice that I have given the blanket form. The child's head has been slightly rounded.

STEP 16 The head will appear to be resting at a three-quarter turn towards the viewer. Shape the head to give this impression. Notice the lines I have drawn to illustrate the planes of the face.

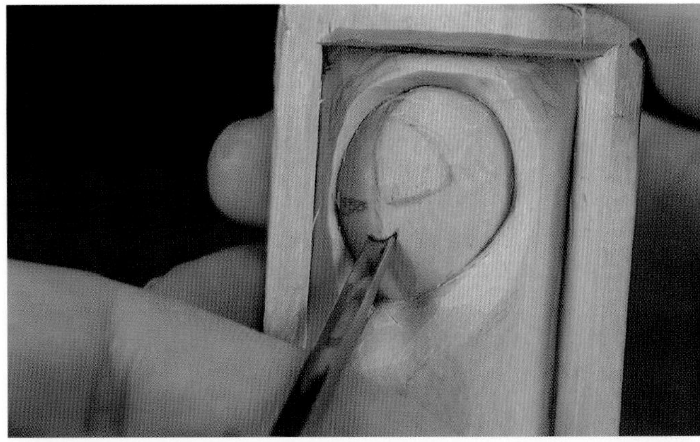

STEP 17 Using a 1/8" shallow gouge, plunge straight in where the nose will be. Refer to the pattern for placement.

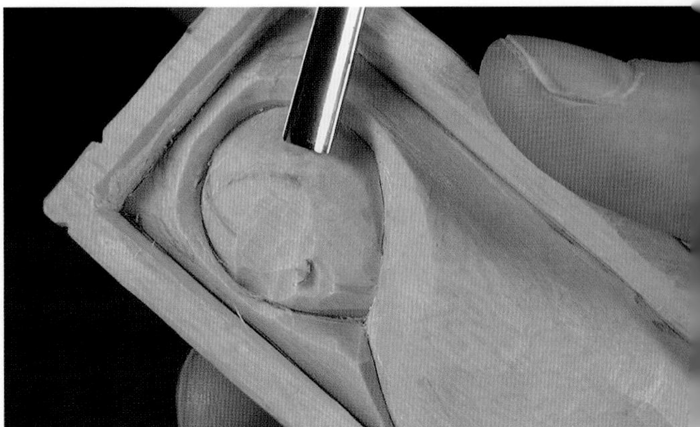

STEP 18 Using a 1/4" shallow gouge, create a hollow representing the nose bridge and eye area. Keep it very shallow!

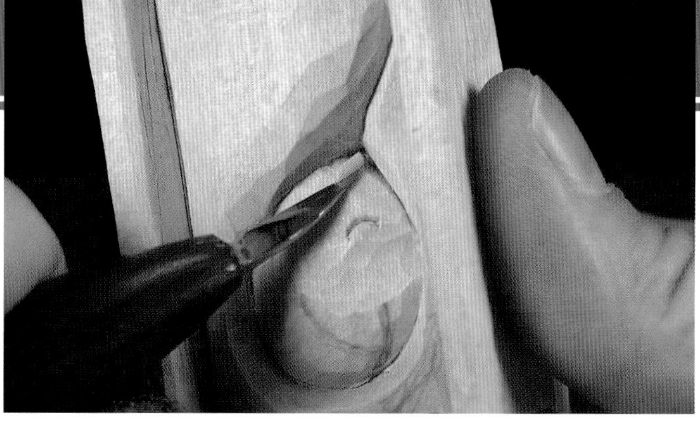

STEP 19 Using your detail knife, pare away small amounts of wood below the nose to help bring it out a little. Shape the nose with the knife as well. Careful, it is very small.

STEP 20 The face shape with the nose finished. I have drawn in the closed eyes and mouth.

STEP 21 Using the detail knife, simply create small v-grooves for the eyes and mouth. These are very minimal features, as a baby's usually are. The mouth opening should be about half the width of the eyes.

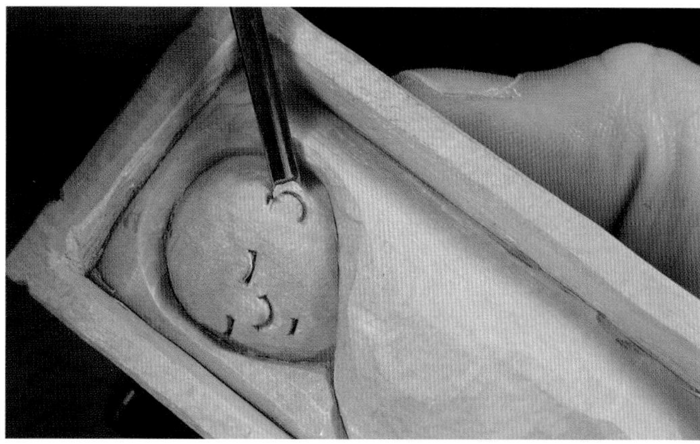

STEP 22 For the one showing ear, keep it simple; outline it with the 1/8" shallow gouge, and pare away a small amount behind it for definition.

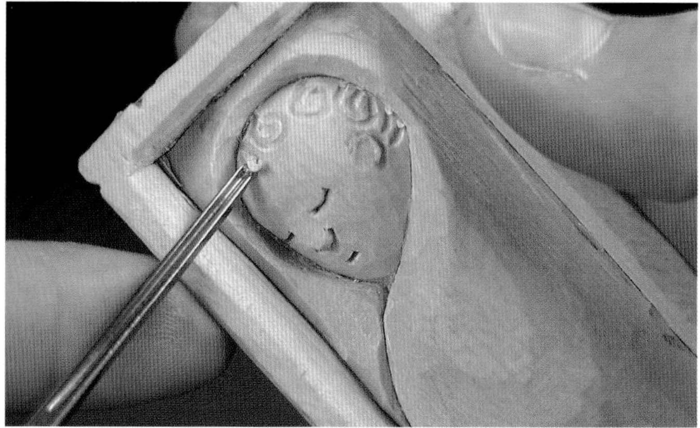

STEP 23 Using a very small veiner gouge, carve in shallow curly-cues for baby hair. Using the same gouge, hollow out the ear a bit.

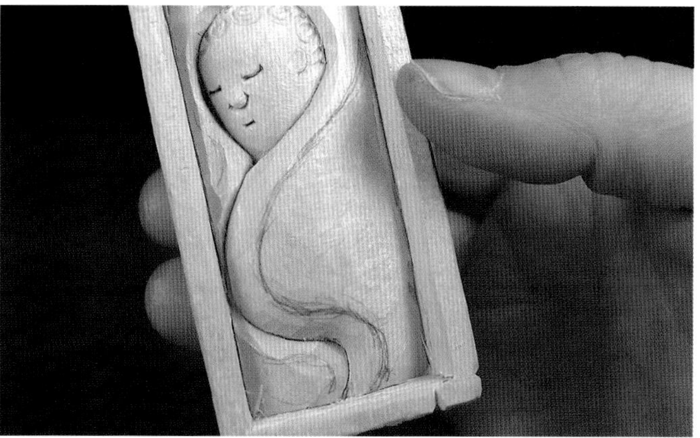

STEP 24 The completed face. Draw in curved lines representing folds in the blanket, as shown.

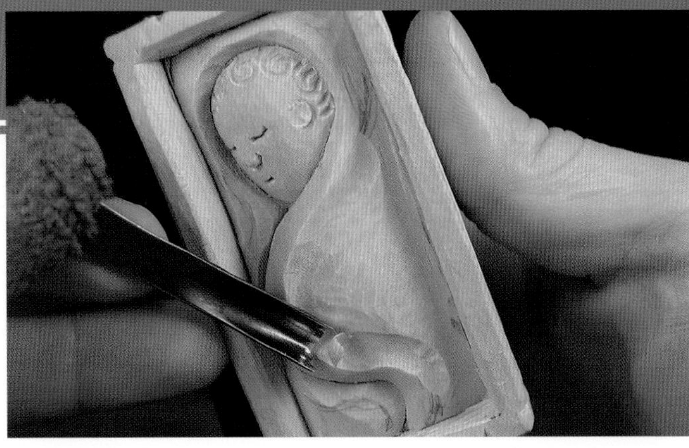

STEP 25 Define these folds with a 1/4" half round gouge.

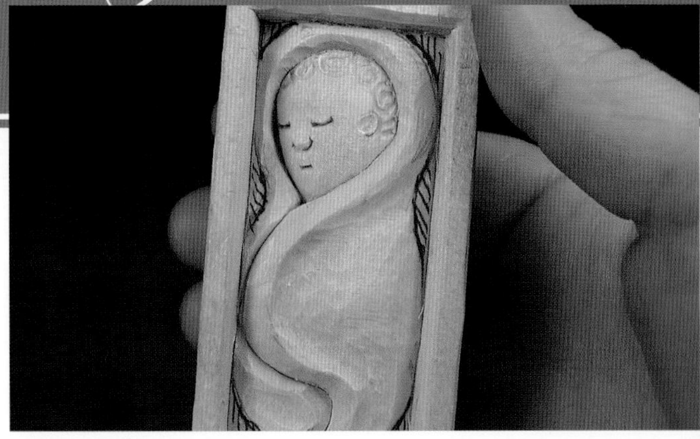

STEP 26 As a final added detail, dig in with the knife around the corners and sides to give the illusion of depth. I have marked the areas to carve as shown.

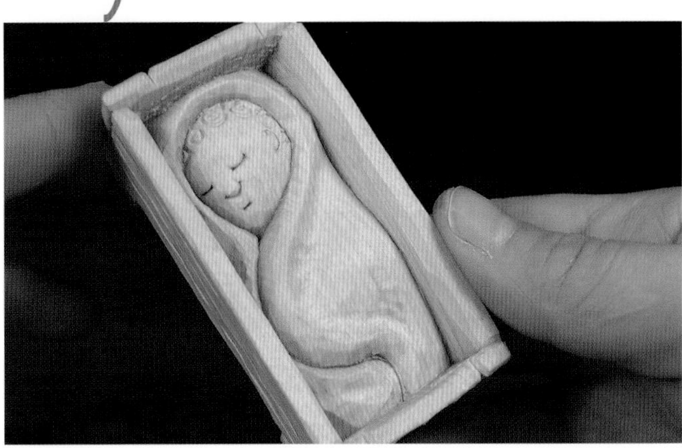

STEP 27 Carving is complete and ready for painting!

Painting The Holy Child

STEP 1 After cleaning, allow the carving to dry. Using the large and small brushes, apply raw sienna to the outside and inner rim of the manger.

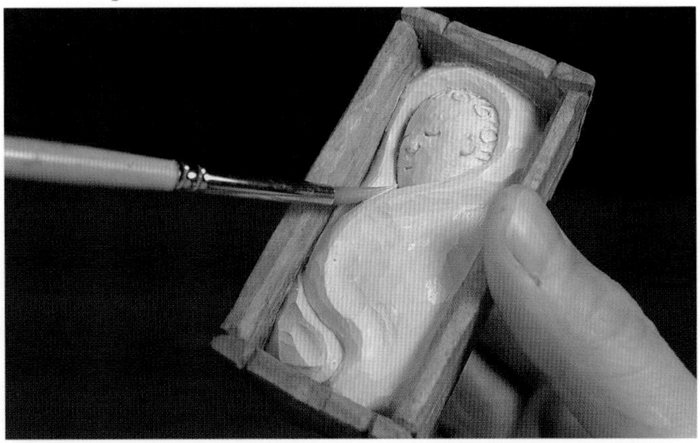

STEP 2 Using the small round brush, paint the blanket antique white.

STEP 3 With the small brush, apply a wash of corn yellow to his hair.

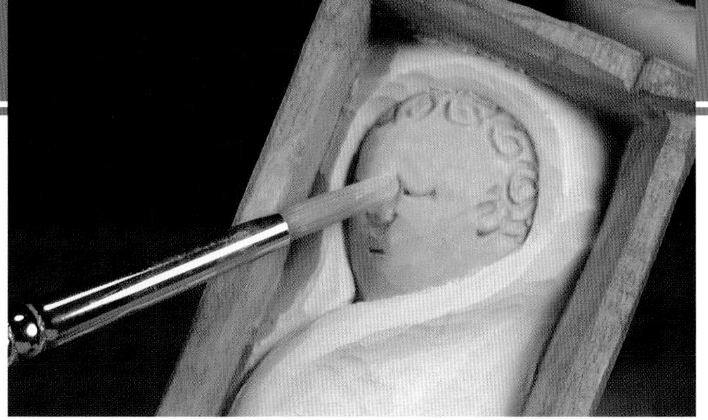

STEP 4 Apply a wash of flesh tone to the face.

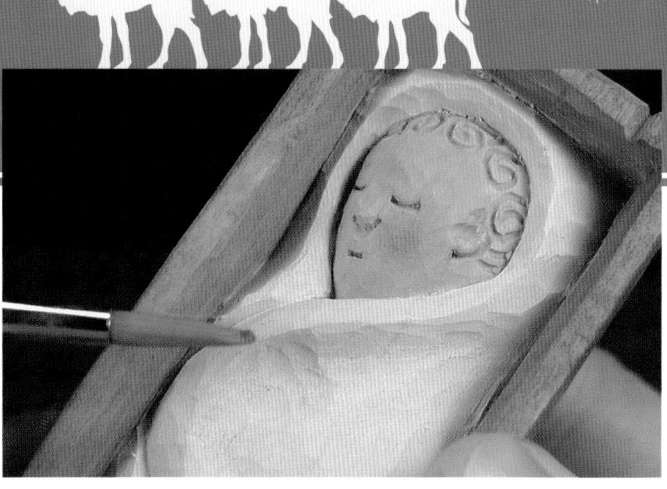

STEP 5 Apply a tiny wash of flesh tone mixed with bright red to his cheek for color.

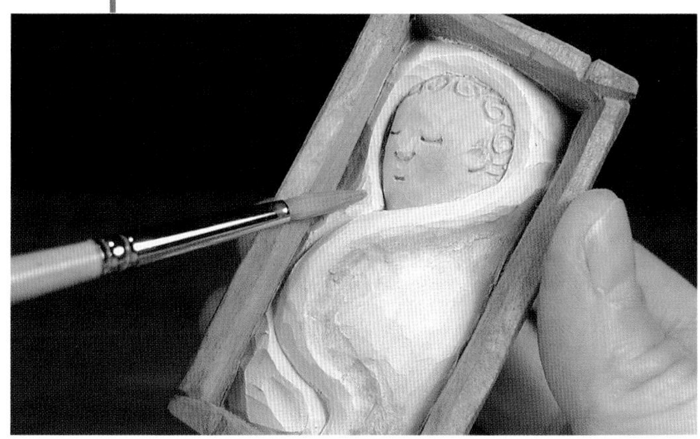

STEP 6 Using the small brush, apply washes of medium gray into the deep areas of the blanket to give it depth. Be sure to blend it in smoothly to the white. Let the carving dry for at least an hour.

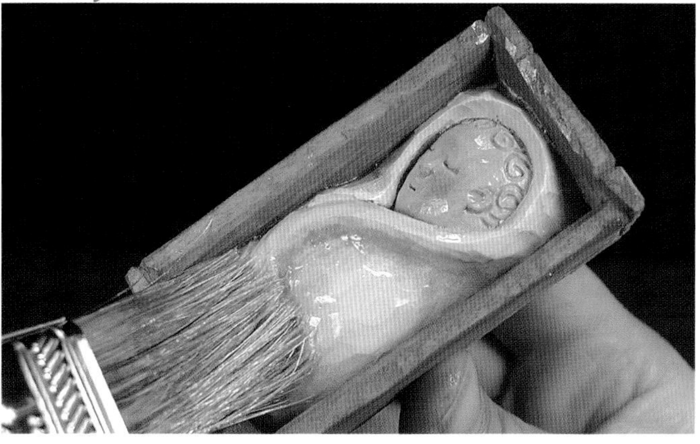

STEP 7 Seal the carving with a thin coat of satin polyurethane. Let the carving dry overnight.

STEP 8 Apply the antique brown gel stain.

STEP 9 Immediately wipe away the excess stain with a cotton cloth. Let the carving dry overnight before handling.

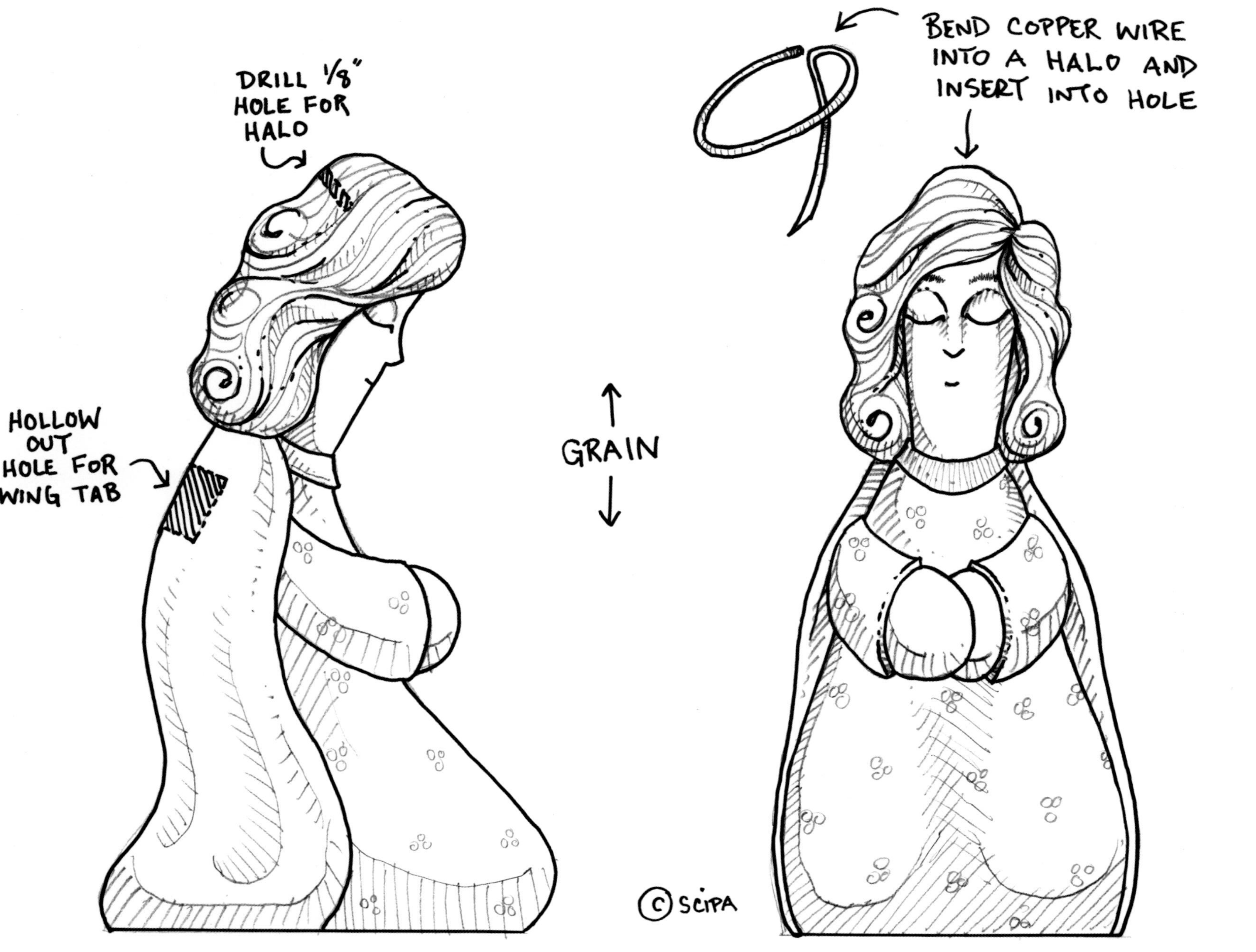
DRILL 1/8" HOLE FOR HALO
HOLLOW OUT HOLE FOR WING TAB
GRAIN
BEND COPPER WIRE INTO A HALO AND INSERT INTO HOLE
© SCIPA
SIDE
FRONT

KNEELING ANGEL

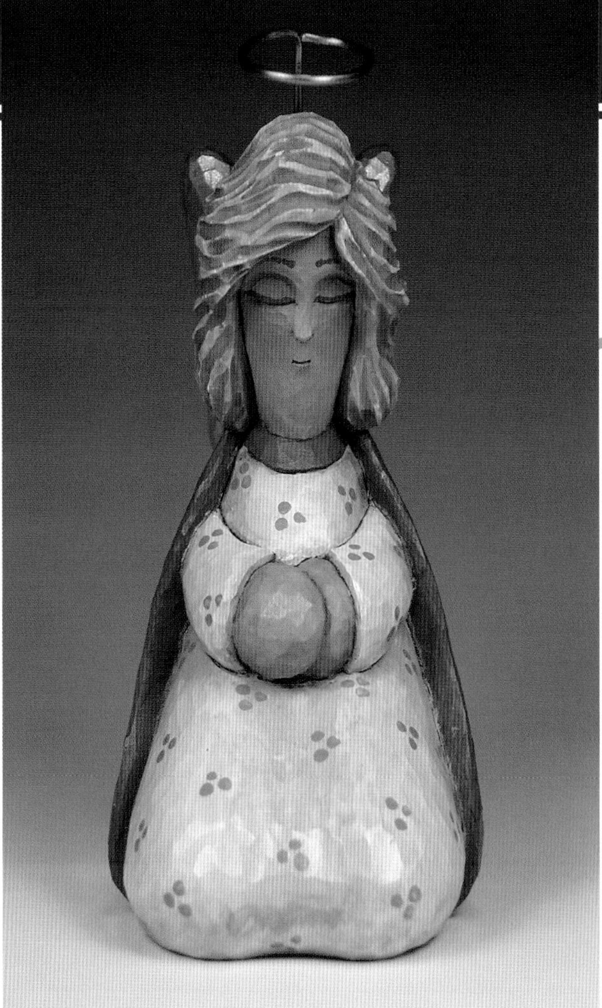

Pattern on Pages 48 & 50

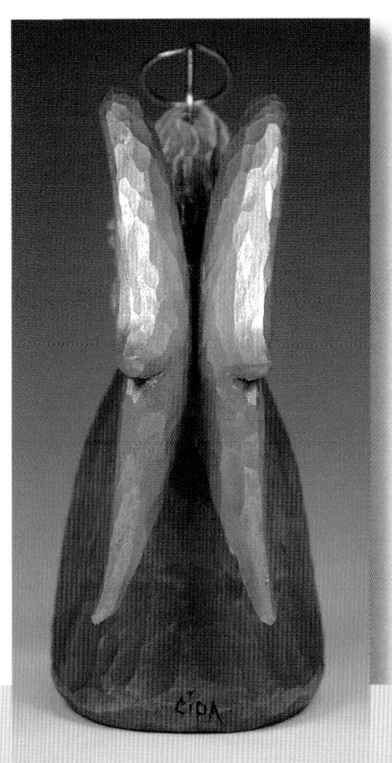

This design was patterned after Mary's, so aside from a few alterations, you should be well prepared to accomplish this carving. Take away the veil, add wings and a halo, and there you have it!

The angel's halo is a piece of 12-gauge copper wire bent to shape and inserted into a 1/8" pre-drilled hole. Hold it in place with a dab of two-part quick drying epoxy. The wings require a bit more attention. They are both carved from a single piece of wood and appear to be in the folded position. If you take a look at the pattern, you will see a view from the rear and the side. Saw out the blank based on the side view and hand-carve the piece to resemble the rear view. Notice the tab insert. This measures about 3/8" thick and about 1/2" long. Using your knife and a small half-round gouge, fashion a hole as shown in the back of the angel to accommodate the tab. Do this only after you have already carved the wings and the tab is in its final shape. Take your time, remove small amounts, and keep fitting the wings until you have a nice snug fit. When you are happy with this, glue it in place with some yellow wood glue. A few rubber bands will help to keep the wing assembly in place until it dries. The block for the angel measures 2 3/4" x 3 1/4" x 6", and the block for the wings measures 1 3/4" x 2" x 4 1/2".

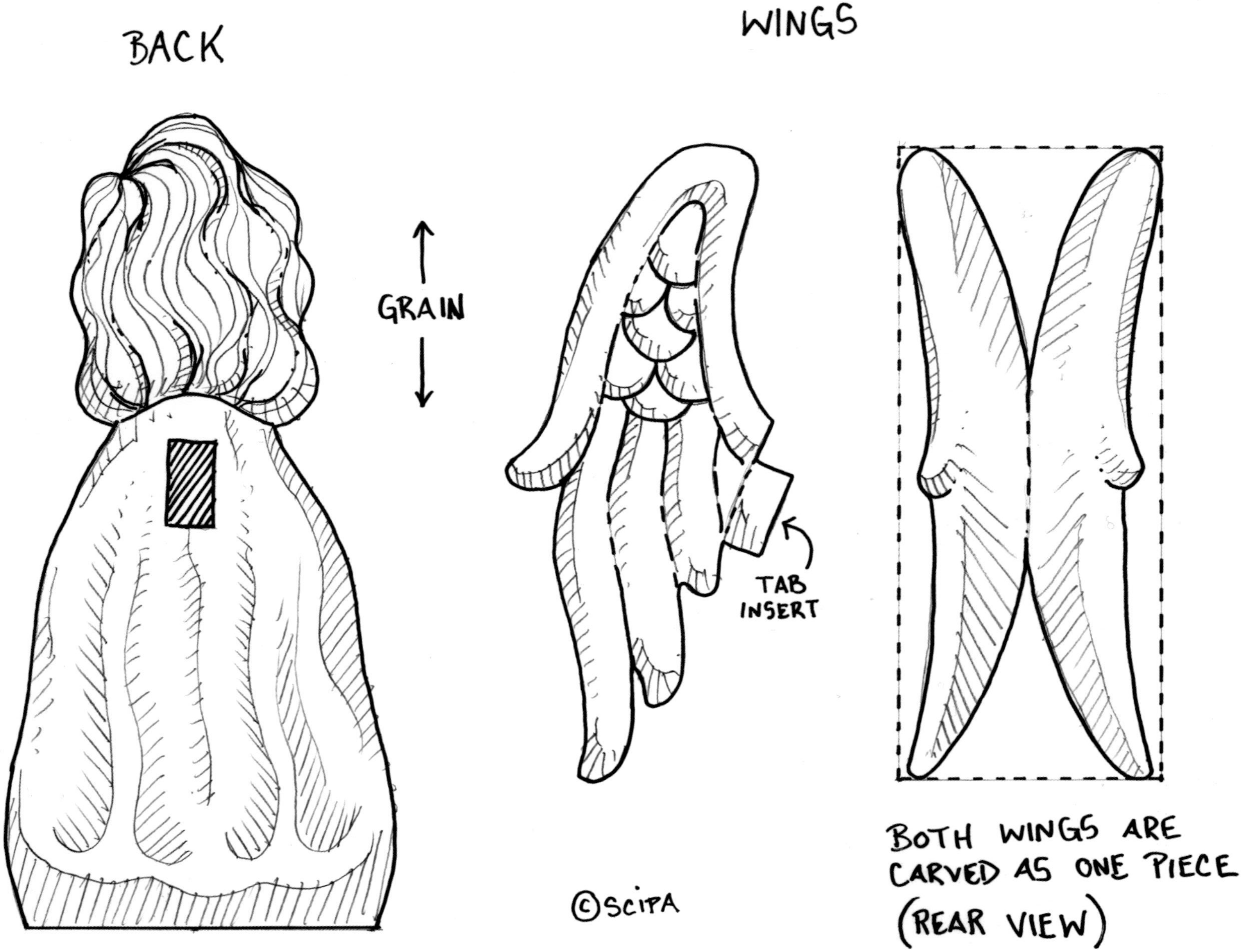

BACK

GRAIN

WINGS

TAB INSERT

©SCIPA

BOTH WINGS ARE CARVED AS ONE PIECE (REAR VIEW)

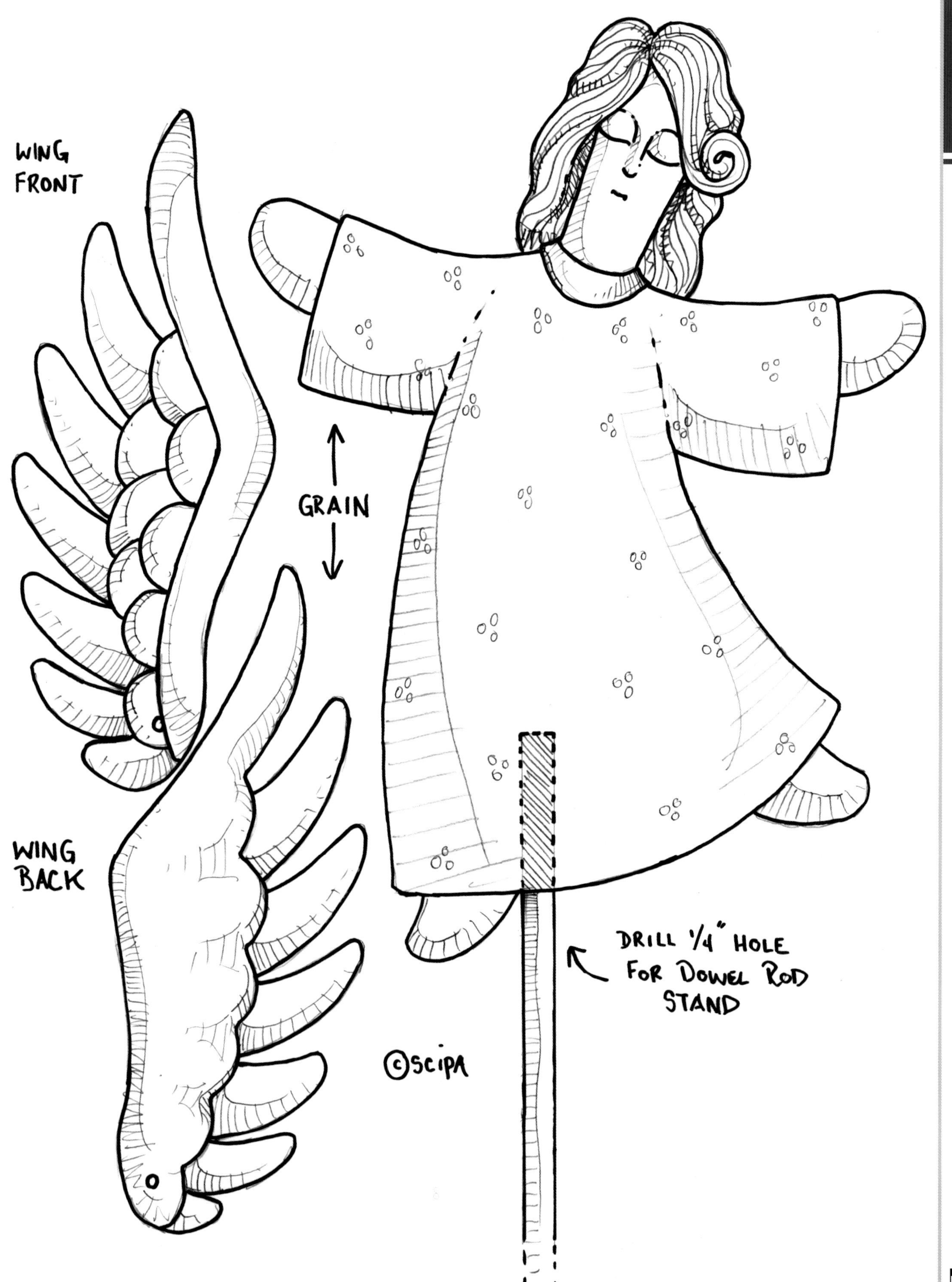
WING FRONT
GRAIN
WING BACK
DRILL 1/4" HOLE FOR DOWEL ROD STAND
©SCIPA

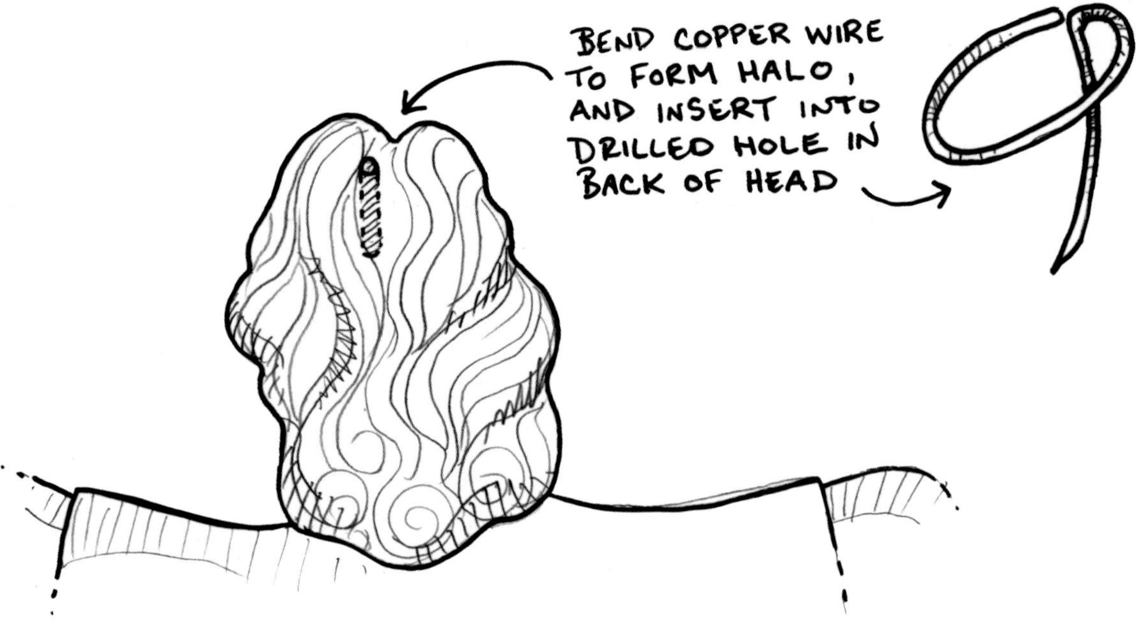

BEND COPPER WIRE
TO FORM HALO,
AND INSERT INTO
DRILLED HOLE IN
BACK OF HEAD

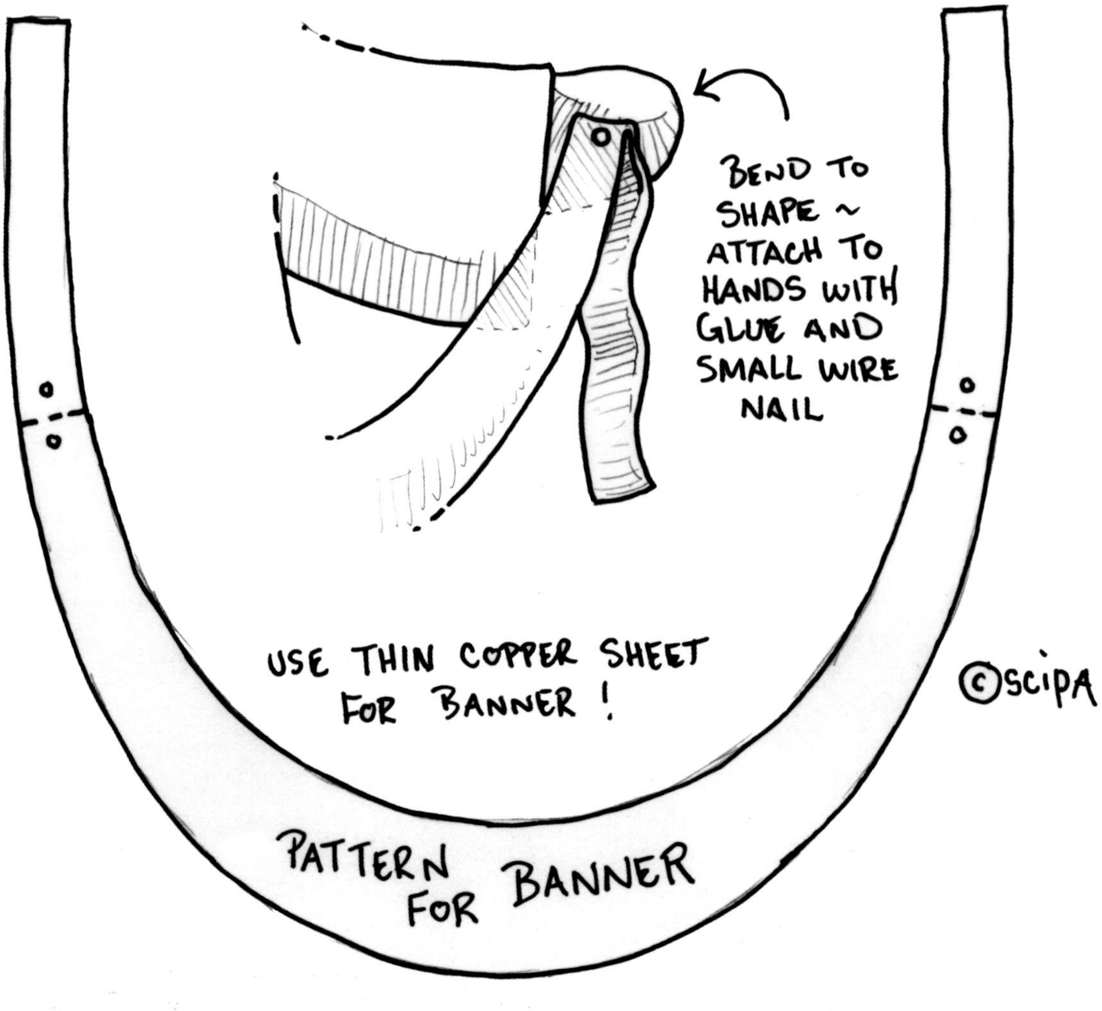

BEND TO
SHAPE ~
ATTACH TO
HANDS WITH
GLUE AND
SMALL WIRE
NAIL

USE THIN COPPER SHEET
FOR BANNER!

PATTERN
FOR BANNER

FLYING ANGEL

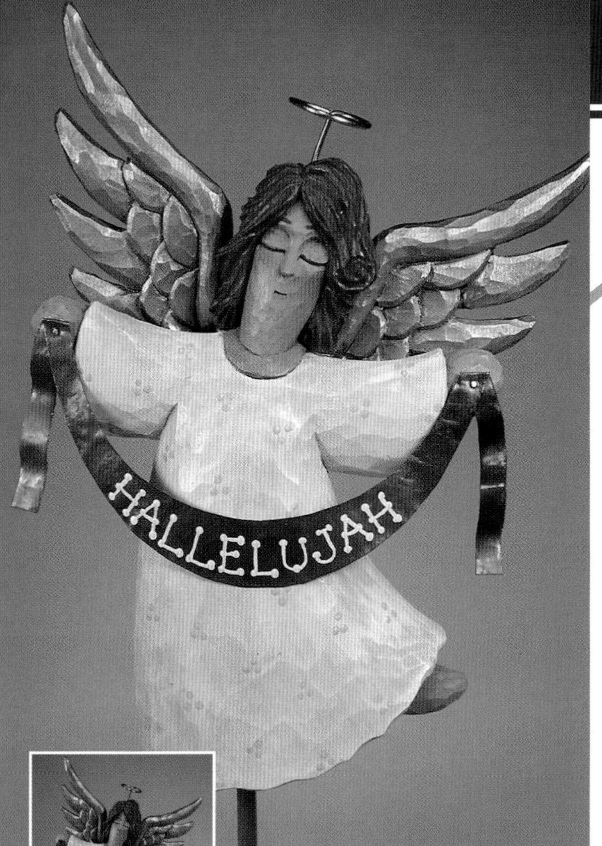

Pattern on Pages 51 & 52

*T*his design is the only one that actually suggests action; the others are more static. The flying angel is meant to be displayed hovering over the whole scene with a proclamation of praise. She is mounted on a 12" long 1/4" dowel rod and supported by a block base measuring 3" x 4 1/2" x 1 1/2". The support remains unpainted to keep it low key. Drill 1/4" holes in the angel and the base, but do not glue the dowel in place. It is better to just have it fit snugly so you can disassemble the carving for storage. I have not provided a side or back view pattern of this angel because there is really not much to show. Study the photos for these views. The block for the body measures 5 1/2" x 2 1/4" x 7 1/2". The wings are carved of 1/2" thick material measuring 2" x 5 1/4" and are attached to the angel's back with glue and small wire nails. Pre-drill the holes for the nails to avoid splitting the wings.

For the banner I used thin copper sheeting. Copper is very easy to work. You can cut it with tin snips and antique it by heating it with a common plumbing torch. Be very careful when doing this; you may want to consult with someone who has experience in using a plumbing torch. If this is something you don't want to deal with, try using a nice heavy paper or card stock. Bend the banner to shape and coat it thinly with polyurethane to stiffen it. The lettering is simply painted with acrylic paint and a fine detail brush. Don't forget the halo!

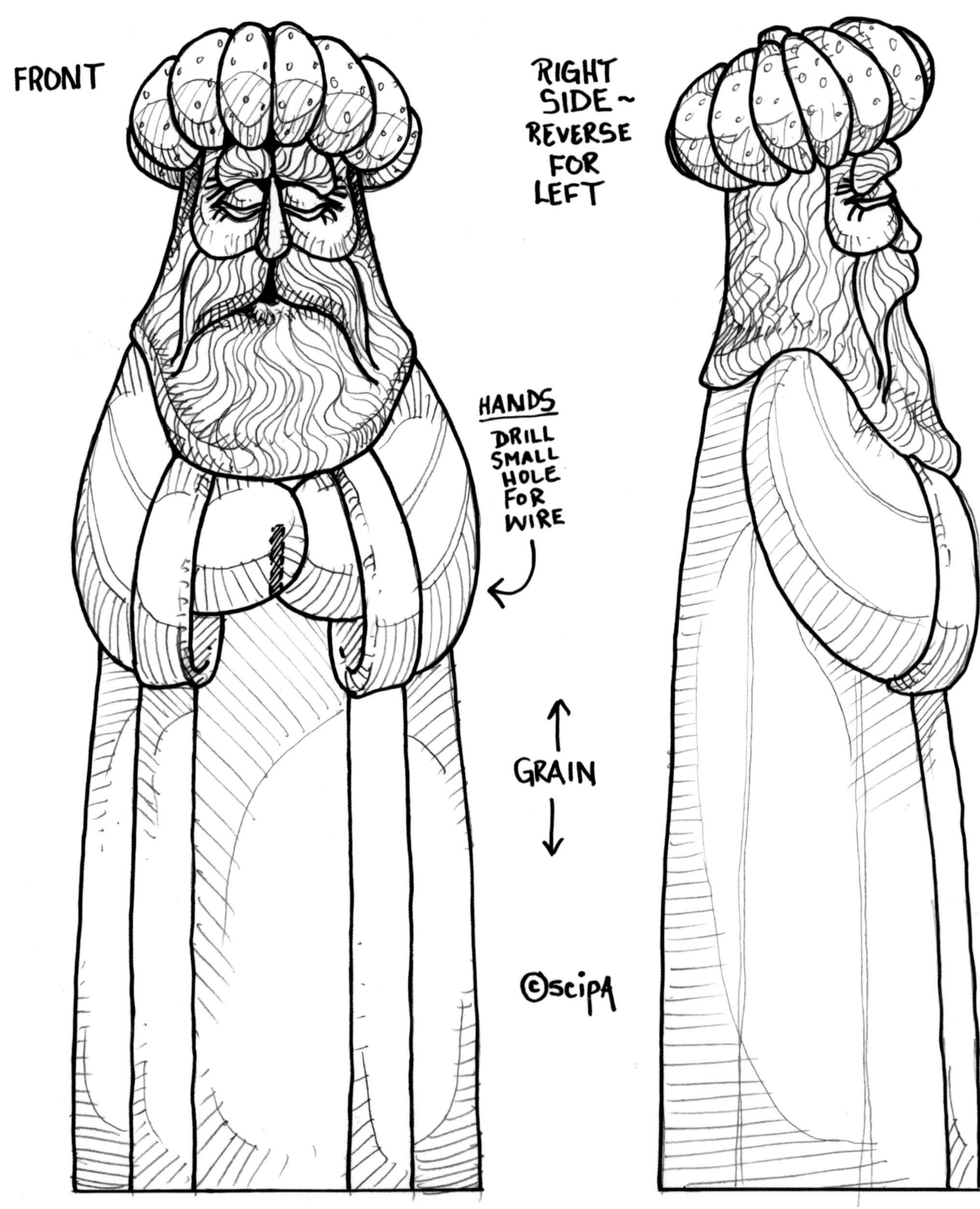
FRONT
RIGHT SIDE~ REVERSE FOR LEFT
HANDS
DRILL SMALL HOLE FOR WIRE
GRAIN
©scipA

CASPAR BEARING FRANKINCENSE

Pattern on Pages 54 & 56

Caspar is one of the three kings, or wisemen. He has come bearing the gift of frankincense, an aromatic tree resin native to East Africa. Frankincense was highly valued by royalty in the ancient world. It is still available today and is used for medicinal, as well as spiritual, purposes. Here I have Caspar holding a ball-like incense burner, or *censer*. The traditional method for burning the powdered form of frankincense is to place it over live coals within the brass ball, which is suspended by a chain.

This censer is simply constructed from a carved ball with a twisted wire inserted through the center. Flatten one side of the ball just a bit and glue this side to Caspar's body. Insert and glue the chain up into a small hole drilled through his hands. The design of this figure is similar to Joseph's, with the exception of the turban. Carving the turban can be a little tricky. Whittle out the general shape first, referring closely to the pattern. Then use a v-tool to define the pumpkin-like segments. Finally, I painted Caspar to resemble a man of Middle Eastern descent. You may paint him as you wish. Caspar's robe is traditionally blue. The block measures 3" x 2 1/2" x 8". The censer is carved from a block measuring 1" x 1".

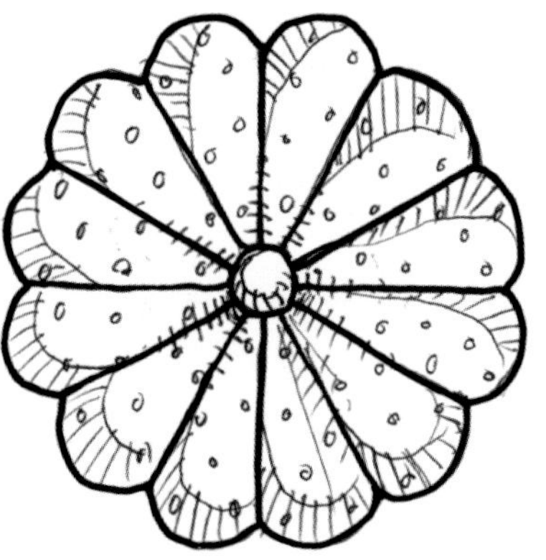
TOP VIEW OF TURBAN

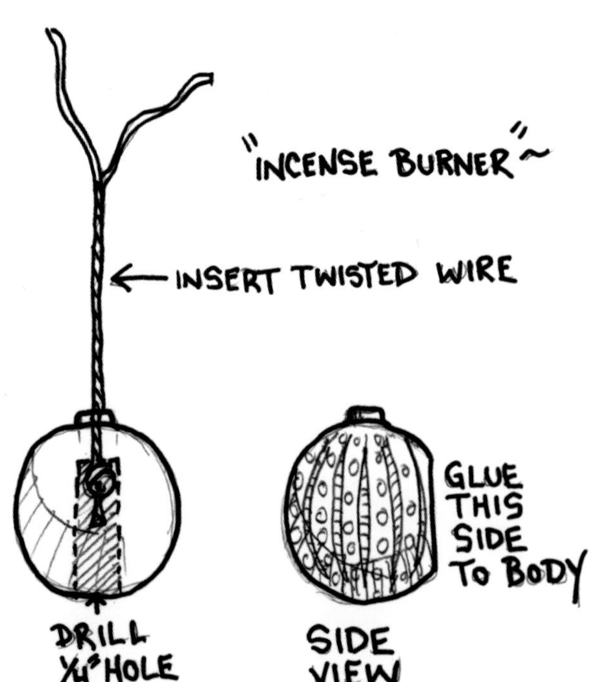

FRONT
RIGHT SIDE
GRAIN
©scipa

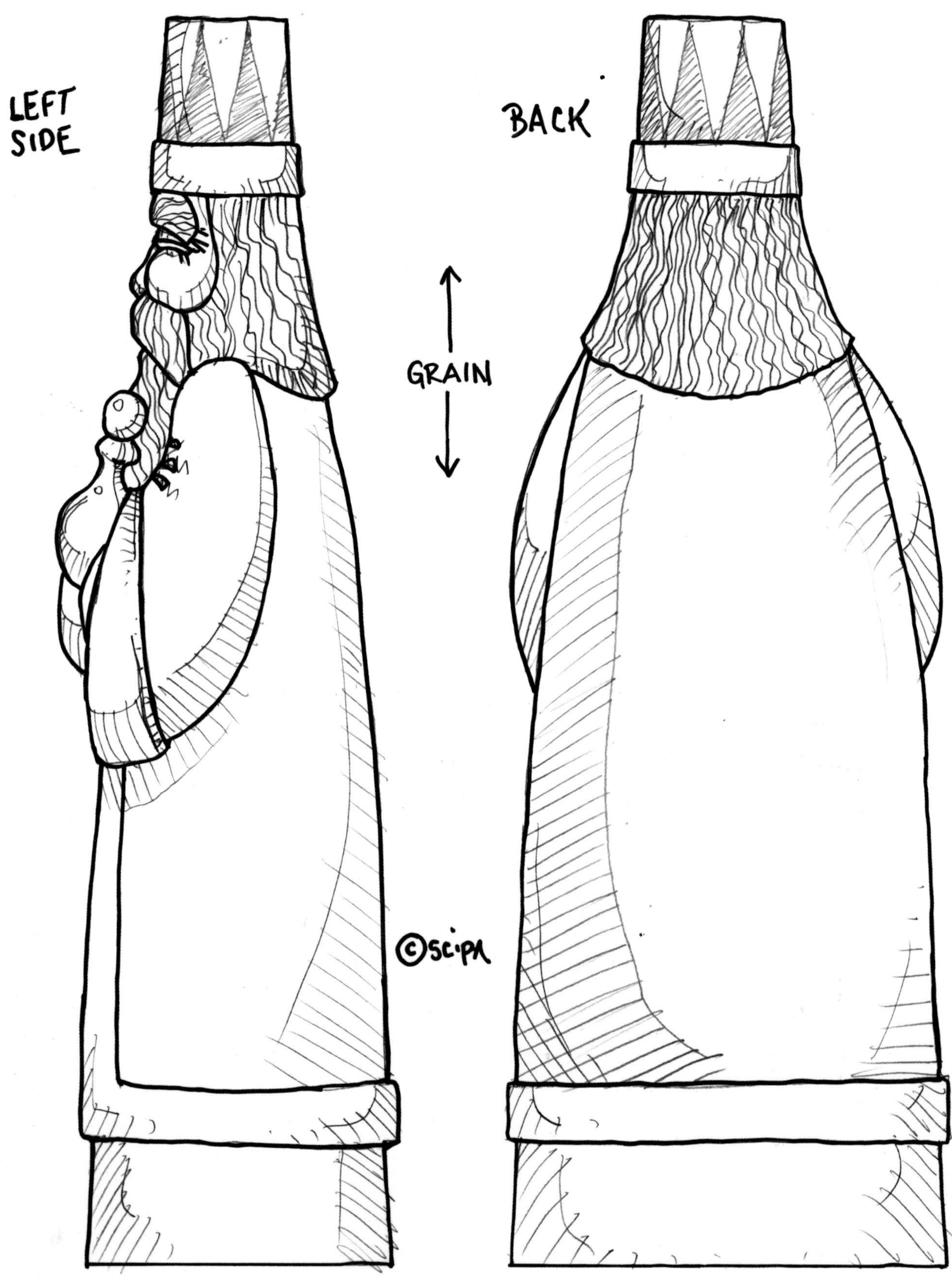
LEFT SIDE
BACK
GRAIN
©scipa

MELCHIOR BEARING MYRRH

Pattern on Pages 57 & 58

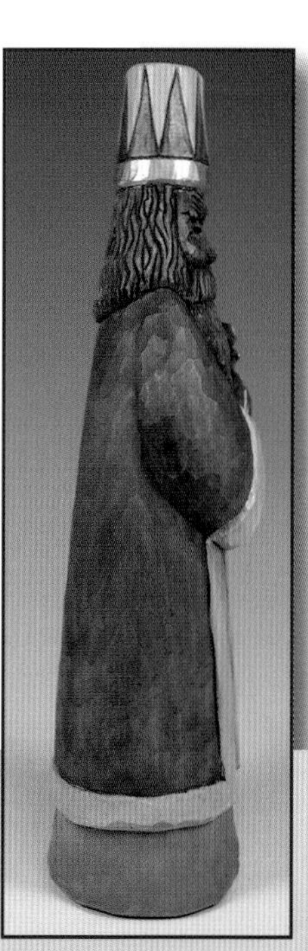

Melchior, the second of the three kings, comes bearing myrrh. Like frankincense, myrrh is also an aromatic resin native to East Africa and southern Arabia. Both spices have always been associated with each other and are used for the same purposes. However, myrrh is more mysterious and was once one of the most desired and sought after items in the world! The Egyptians and Hebrews both used it long before the Holy birth ever took place. Myrrh was often converted into liquid form and used as an anointing oil.

Here, Melchior is holding a decanter of the precious oil. This carving design is very similar to Joseph's and should be fairly easy to complete. Melchior's robes are traditionally green. I painted his skin dark, suggesting African or Egyptian descent. The block measures 3" x 2 $^1/_2$" x 8 $^1/_2$".

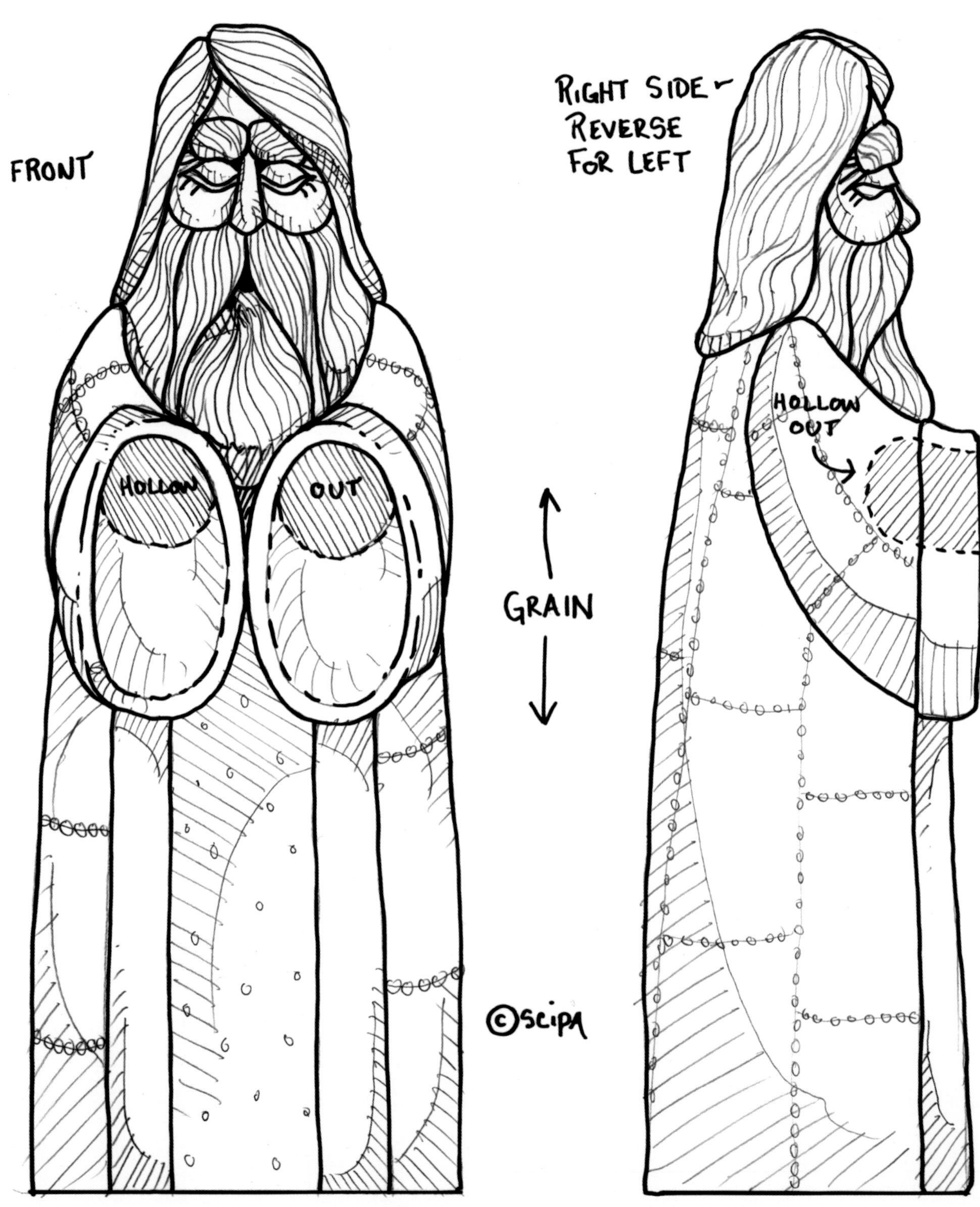
FRONT
HOLLOW
OUT
RIGHT SIDE - REVERSE FOR LEFT
HOLLOW OUT
GRAIN
©SCIPA

BALTHAZAR BEARING GOLD

Pattern on Pages 60 & 62

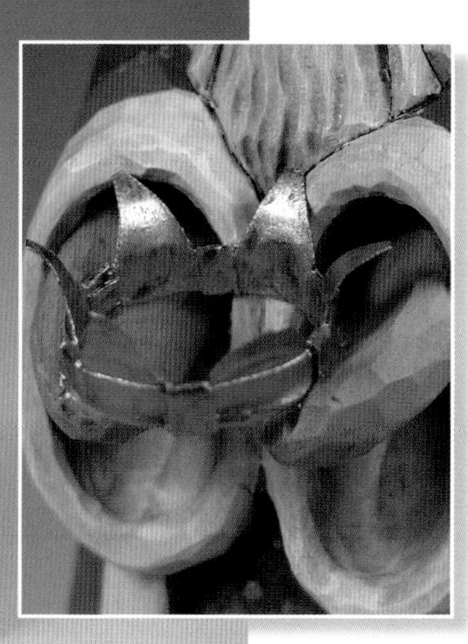

Balthazar, the third of the three kings, comes bearing the gift of gold. I chose the gold to be in the form of a crown, as if Balthazar is offering his own in tribute to the newborn king. Actually, during my research, I found that it is likely the three travelers weren't kings at all, but rather wisemen—men of worldly knowledge, probably astrologers who discovered the star that led them to Bethlehem. There are lots of different theories. In any case, it is a noble and symbolic idea that kings from other lands came to pay homage to this tiny baby.

In order to have Balthazar holding up the crown, I chose to add his hands for strength. Once the figure is carved, hollow out the areas indicated on the pattern. Carve the hands separately, as shown; then glue them in place. For the crown, I used copper sheeting painted gold. A cutout pattern is provided. Simply trace the pattern onto the copper, cut it out with tin snips, and bend the crown to shape. Paint the crown with gold acrylic paint. Another option is to use heavy paper or card stock. Once painted and sealed with polyurethane, the paper crown will become stiff and durable. You could also carve a crown, but it will be very fragile.

Be sure to glue the crown to Balthazar's hands as a very last step; otherwise it will be difficult to paint his hands, let alone seal and antique them. Balthazar's robe is traditionally red. I painted his skin light. The block measures 3" x 2 $^1/_2$" x 8". The hands are carved of $^1/_2$" x 1 $^1/_2$" blocks.

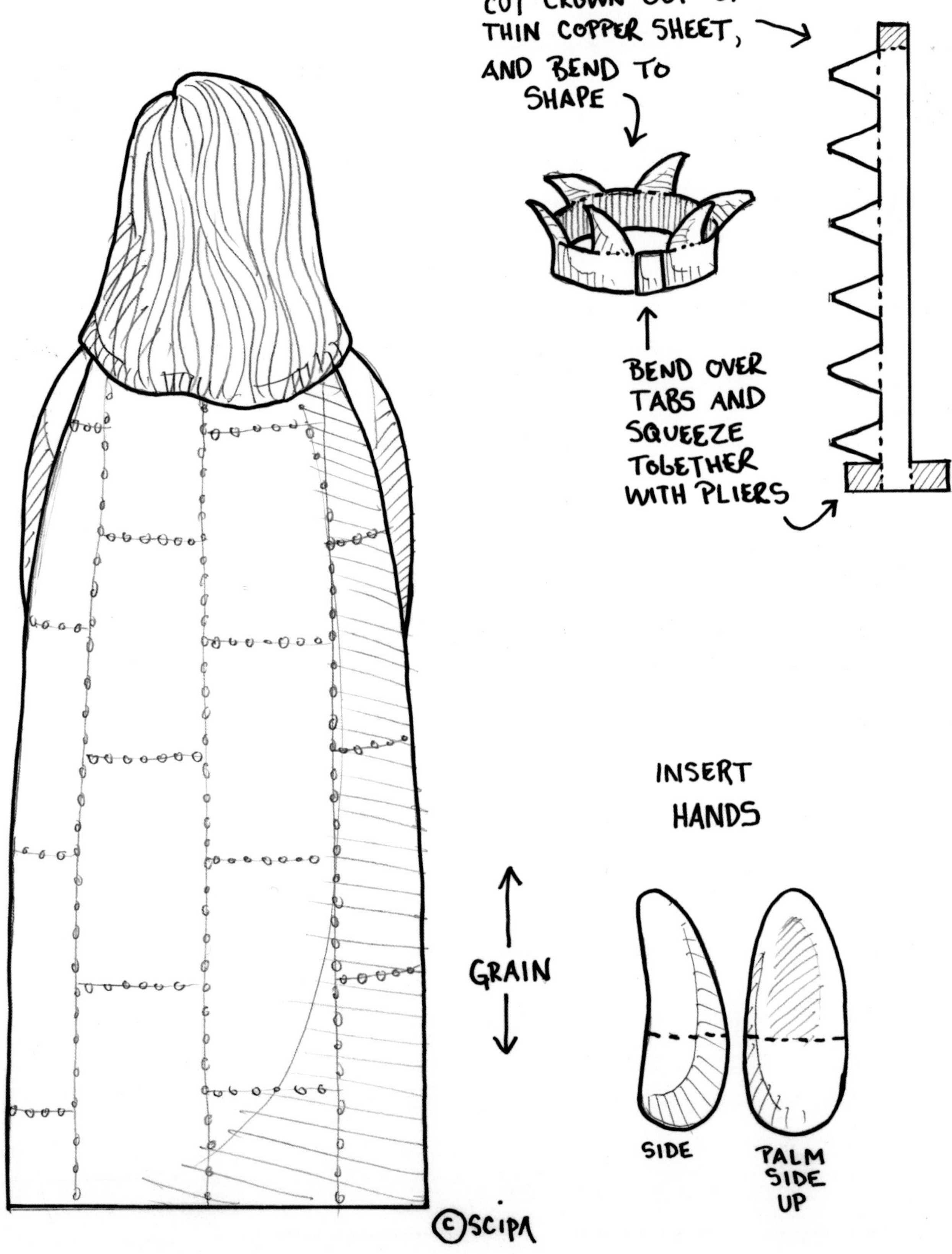
CUT CROWN OUT OF
THIN COPPER SHEET,
AND BEND TO
SHAPE
BEND OVER
TABS AND
SQUEEZE
TOGETHER
WITH PLIERS
INSERT
HANDS
GRAIN
SIDE
PALM
SIDE
UP
©SCIPA

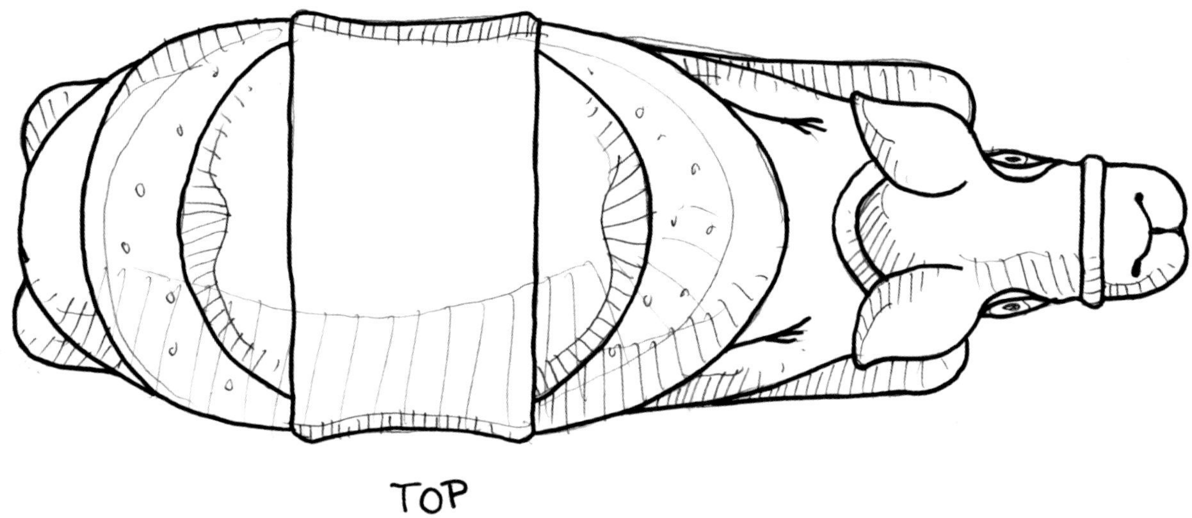

GRAIN

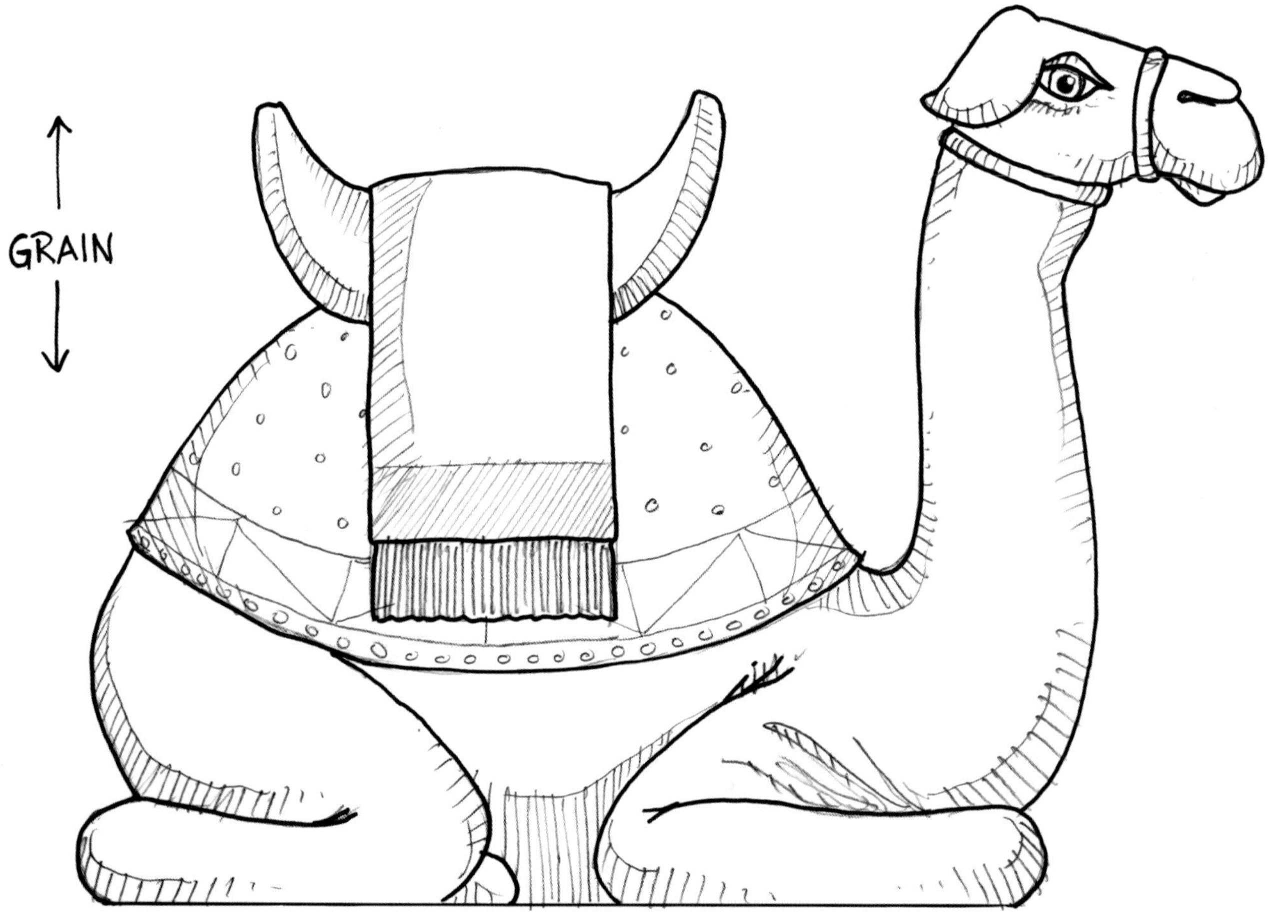

SIDE

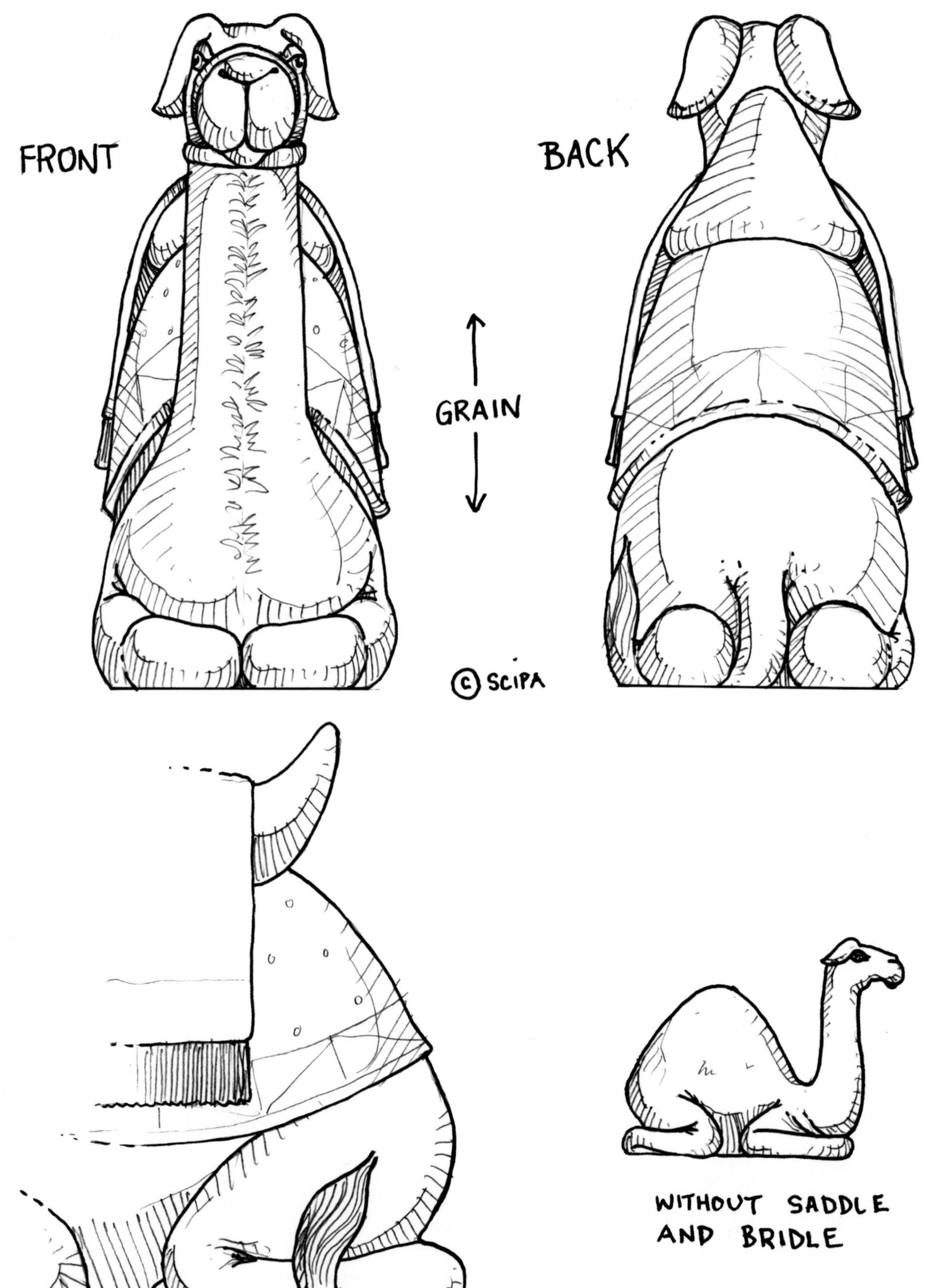
FRONT
BACK
GRAIN
© SCIPA
LEFT SIDE
TO SHOW TAIL
WITHOUT SADDLE
AND BRIDLE

CAMEL

Pattern on Pages 63 & 64

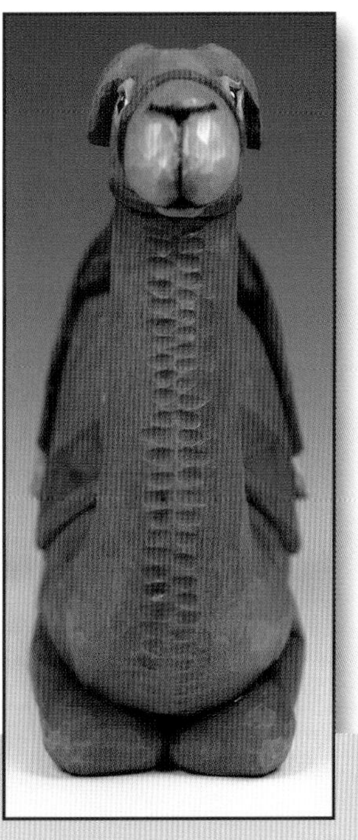

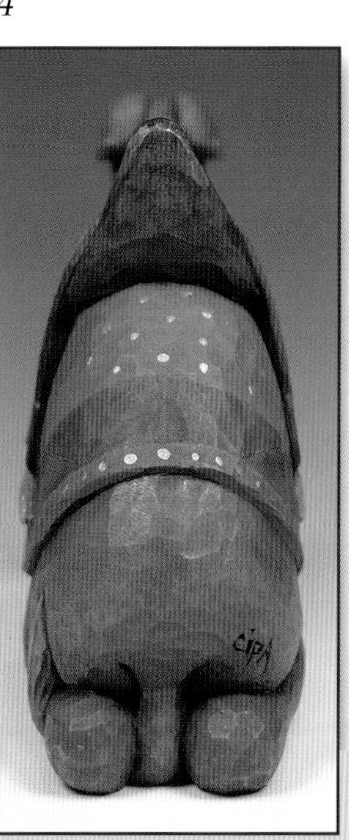

All the animals in this book are carved in the seated position. This is to make them easier to carve and help to reinforce the feeling of reverence. The camel in particular would dominate the scene if it were standing. Although the shape of this carving is rather simple, the grain direction changes a lot due to the presence of the saddle gear. If this is something you don't want, simply eliminate it and the bridle. The camel's legs fold up in a completely different manner than the other animals. Study the patterns closely when carving them. Don't forget to add the tail to one side, as shown. I have left the eyes open on the camel as an option. A camel's eyes tend to be heavy-lidded, as if he were about to nod off. You can easily carve them closed if you wish. The block measures 6 1/2" x 2 1/2" x 4 3/4".

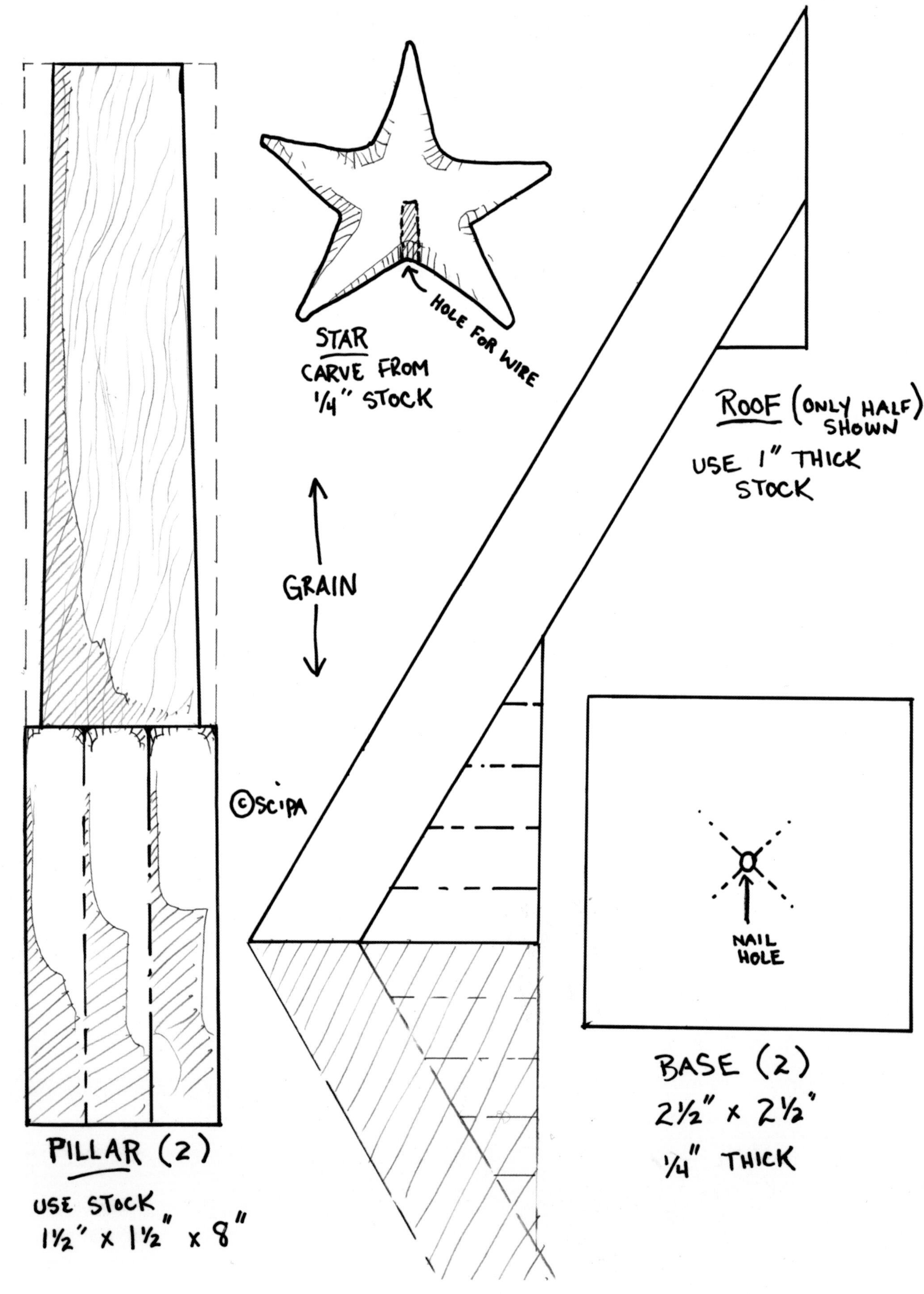
STAR
CARVE FROM
1/4" STOCK
HOLE FOR WIRE
ROOF (ONLY HALF)
SHOWN
USE 1" THICK
STOCK
GRAIN
©SCIPA
NAIL
HOLE
BASE (2)
2½" x 2½"
1/4" THICK
PILLAR (2)
USE STOCK
1½" x 1½" x 8"

STABLE

Pattern on Pages 66 & 68

*T*his design takes some work to complete. You will carve as well as construct. I have kept the construction to a minimum in order to make it simple to understand for those with no experience in this area. The two pillars are carved from solid blocks that measure 1 1/2" x 1 1/2" x 8". Band-saw the gradual taper on all four sides, as shown in the pattern. I have textured the tapered sections with a 1/8" half-round gouge to simulate weathered wood. The lower half is carved to resemble vertical planks. The roof section is sawed out of 1" stock and is 14" long. The center portion is carved to look like vertical planks, while the beams are textured with a shallow gouge to simulate a rough-hewn look. The two bases are cut from 1/4" thick stock and are beveled on the edges with a knife. The Star of Bethlehem is carved from 1/4"-thick stock. I have drilled a small hole in the bottom of the star to accept a piece of 12-gauge copper wire as a support that connects to the peak of the roof. Assembly is clearly illustrated on the diagram provided. Use glue and finish nails. Be sure to pre-drill all the holes. I would suggest assembling both of the bases and the roof all at once, so that the stable can stand in position and dry. That way you can make sure the stable will stand straight and flat when completed.

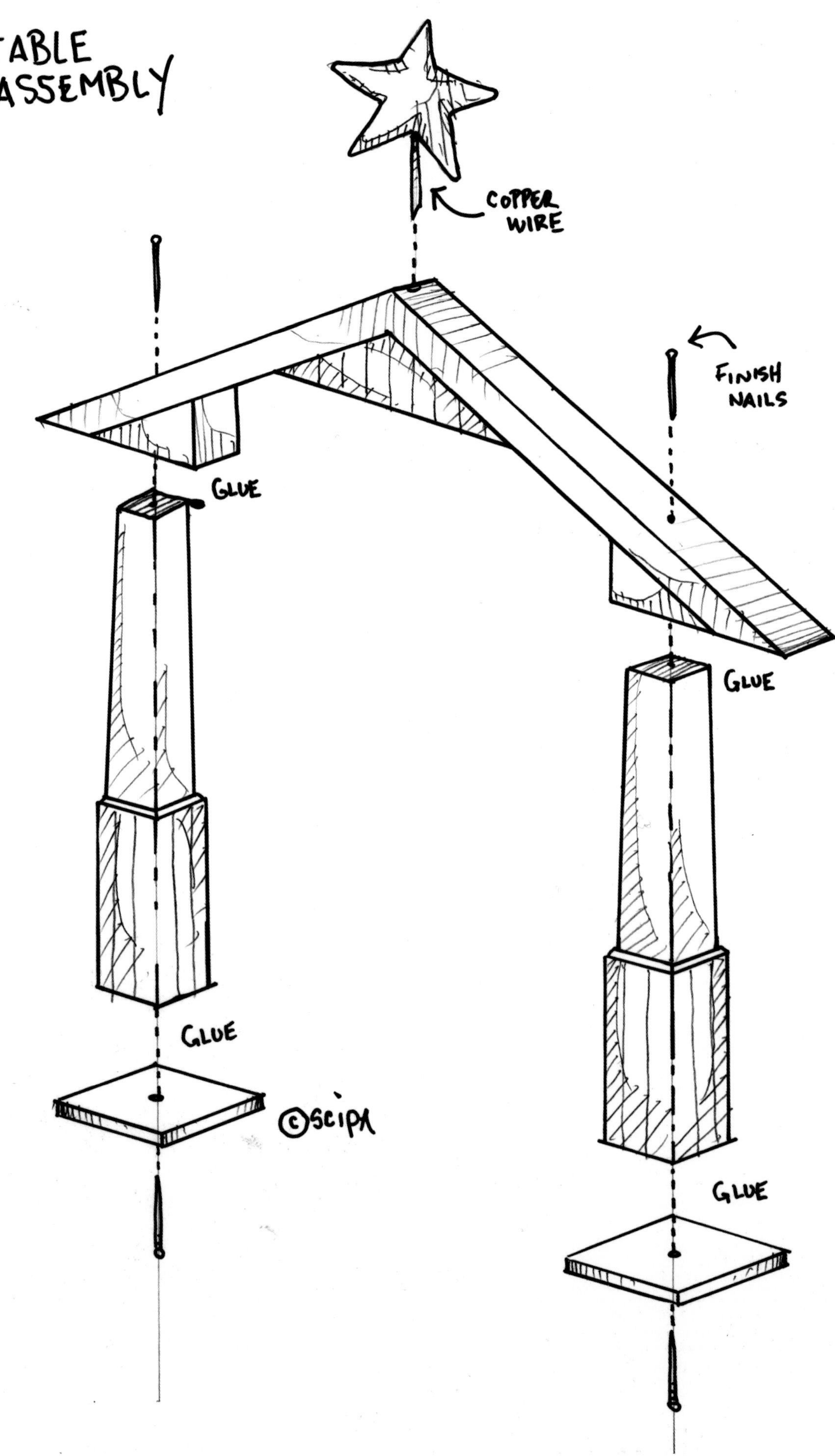
STABLE
ASSEMBLY
COPPER
WIRE
FINISH
NAILS
GLUE
GLUE
GLUE
GLUE
©SCIPA

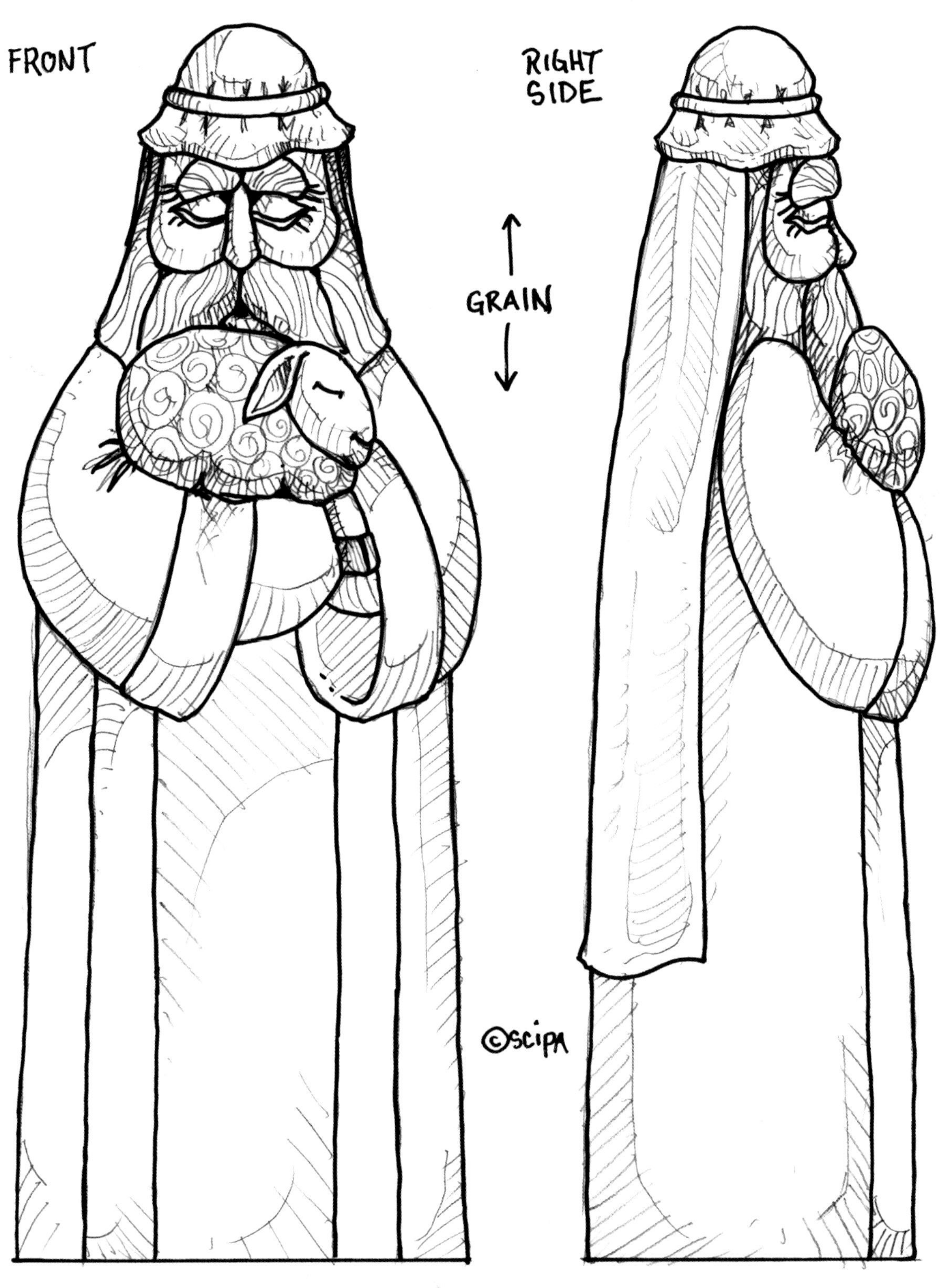
FRONT
RIGHT SIDE
GRAIN
©SCIPA

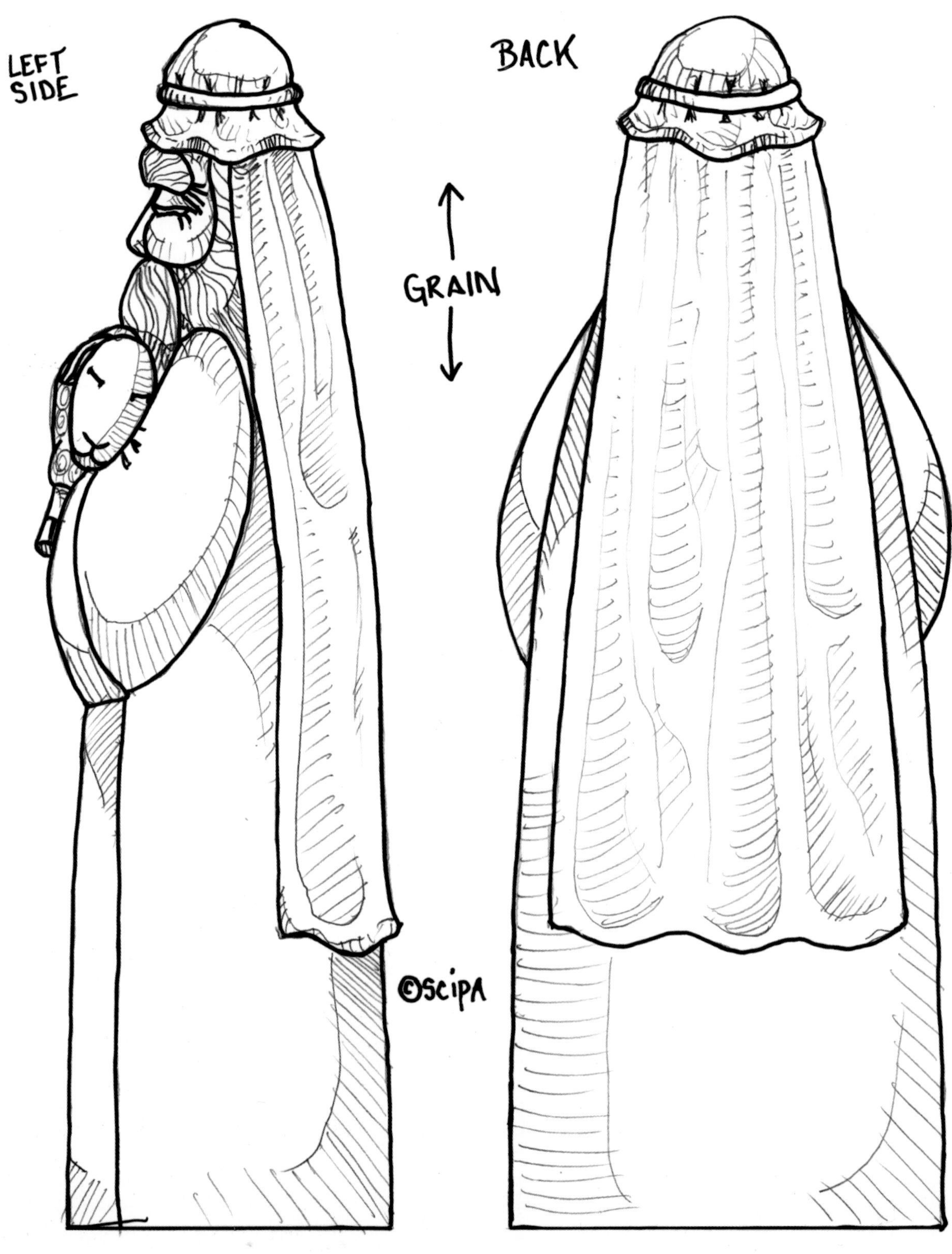
LEFT SIDE
BACK
GRAIN
©SCIPA

SHEPHERD WITH LAMB

Pattern on Pages 69 & 70

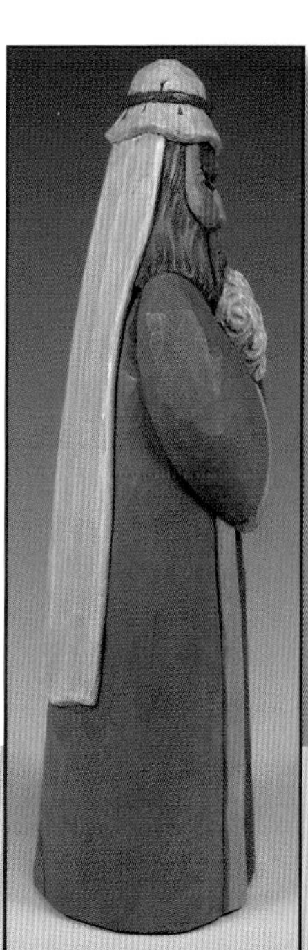

***T**his design is almost identical to Joseph's, with the exception of the lamb in his arms. Be sure to paint him in a color scheme that differs from Joseph's so the two figures are easily distinguishable. The lamb is slightly flattened and is carved almost relief-style. The block measures 3" x 2 1/2" x 8".

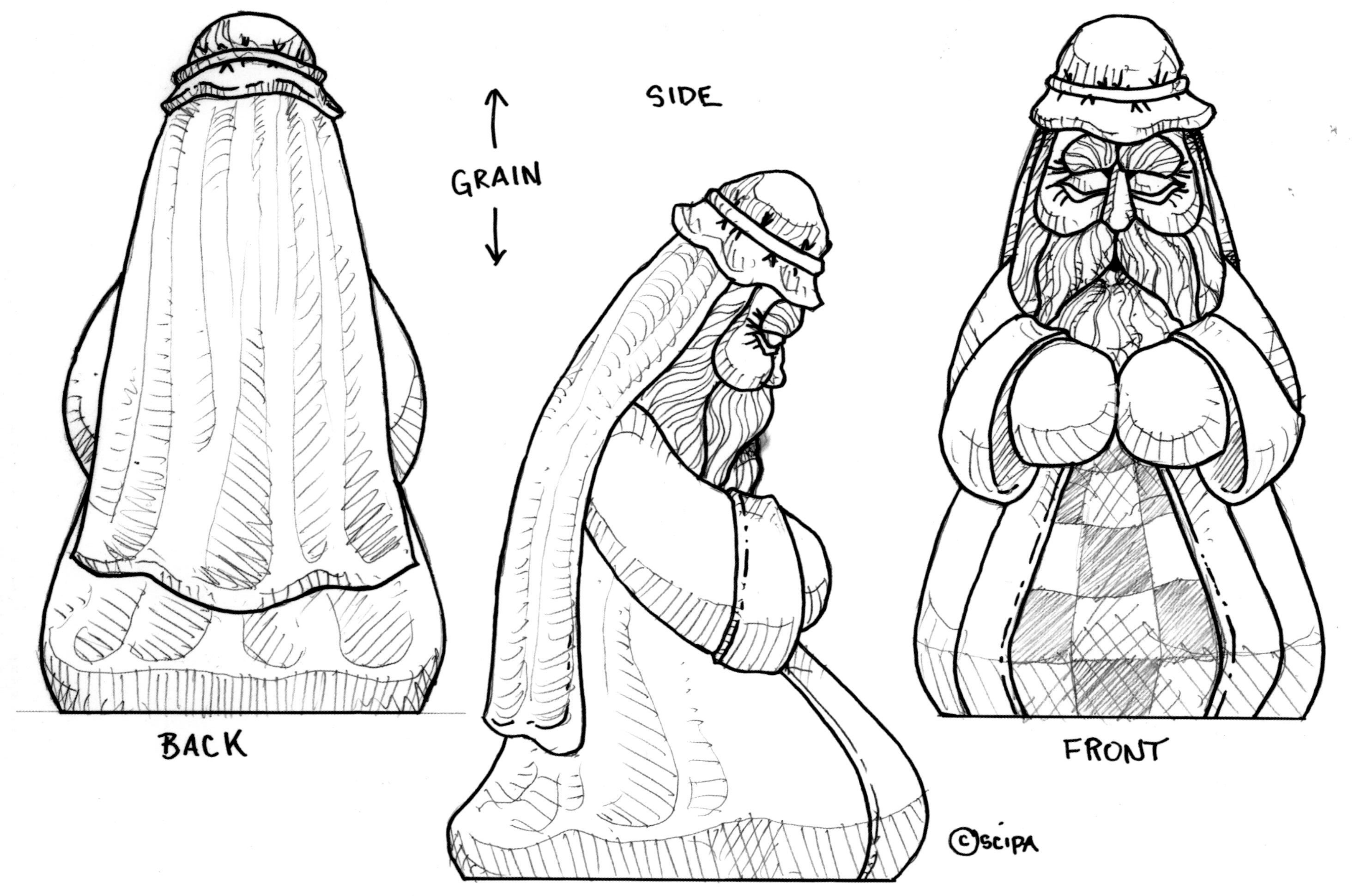
SIDE
GRAIN
BACK
FRONT
©SCIPA

KNEELING SHEPHERD

Pattern on Page 72

This design combines the elements of Joseph's facial features with Mary's kneeling posture. You should be well armed in accomplishing this carving. Paint the shepherd similar to the shepherd holding the lamb to signify that they are akin. Take care when carving this shepherd's face. Because of the bowed position of the head, the grain direction will force you to carve from top to bottom. The block measures 3" x 3 1/2" x 5 1/2".

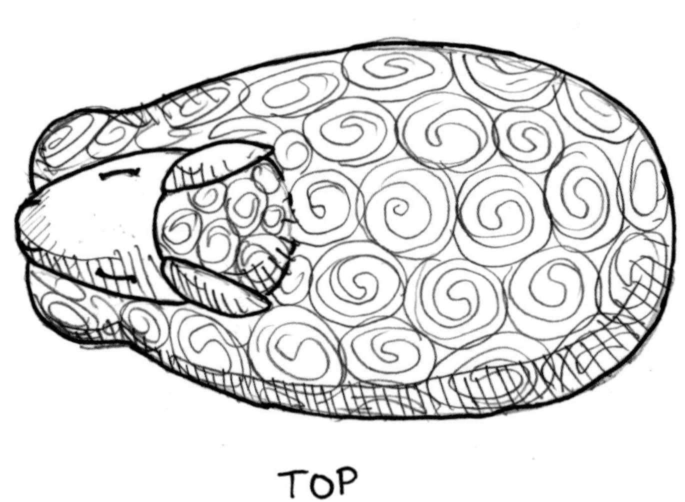

TOP

BACK

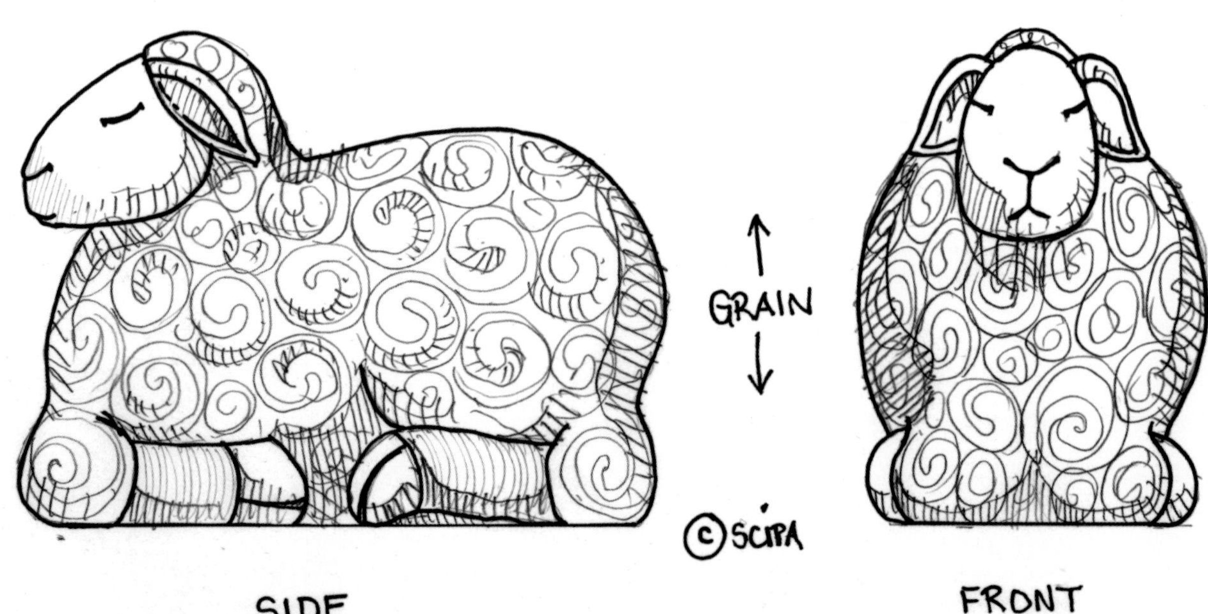

SIDE

FRONT

SHEEP

Pattern on Page 74

***T**he sheep is a simple design but has lots of texture. Accomplish this by carving concentric curly-cues with a 1/8" half-round gouge. Come back with a 1/16" veiner and retrace your marks for more detail. Carve several sheep, some smaller than the others, and place them around the shepherds for interest. The block measures 3 1/2" x 2" x 2 3/4".

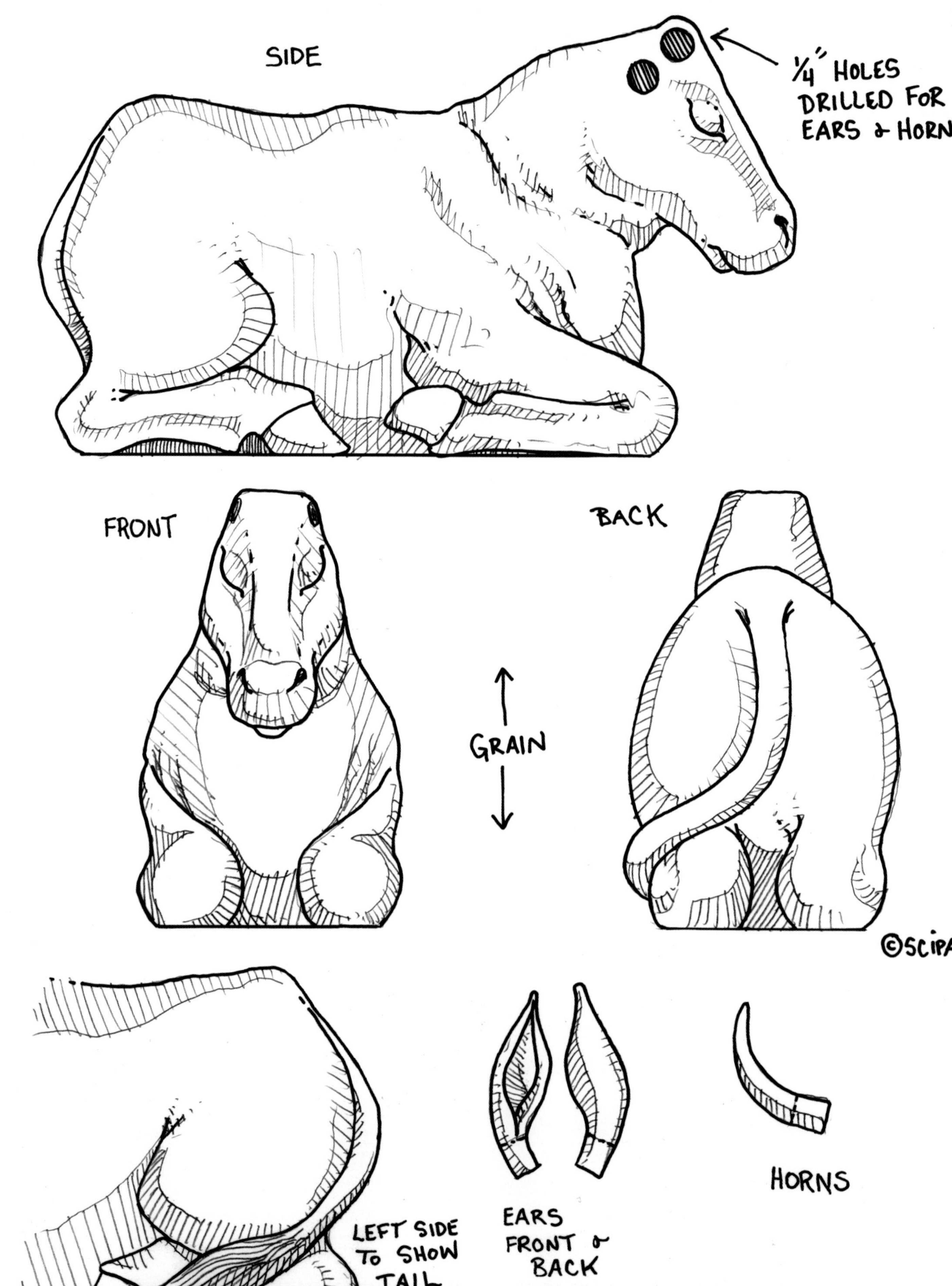
SIDE
1/4" HOLES DRILLED FOR EARS & HORNS
FRONT
BACK
GRAIN
©SCIPA
LEFT SIDE TO SHOW TAIL
EARS FRONT & BACK
HORNS

OX

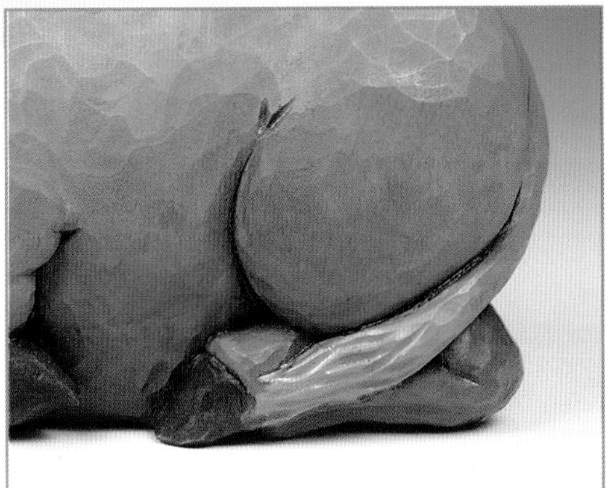

Pattern on Page 76

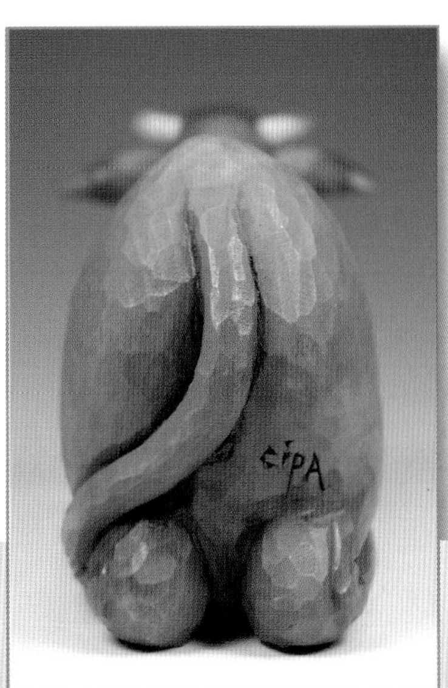

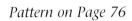

The ox, or bull, is a fairly easy design to carve. I chose to add the ears and the horns separately. If you tried to carve them as one piece, they would most likely snap off due to cross grain. After the ox is carved out, drill 1/4" holes according to the pattern. Once you have carved the ears and horns, simply glue them in place. Be sure to study the photos for correct placement. The horns should be tilted forward, rather than straight up, so they follow the neckline. The block measures 6" x 2 1/4" x 3 1/2". The ears and horns are carved from 1/4"-thick stock. Be sure the grain runs length-wise.

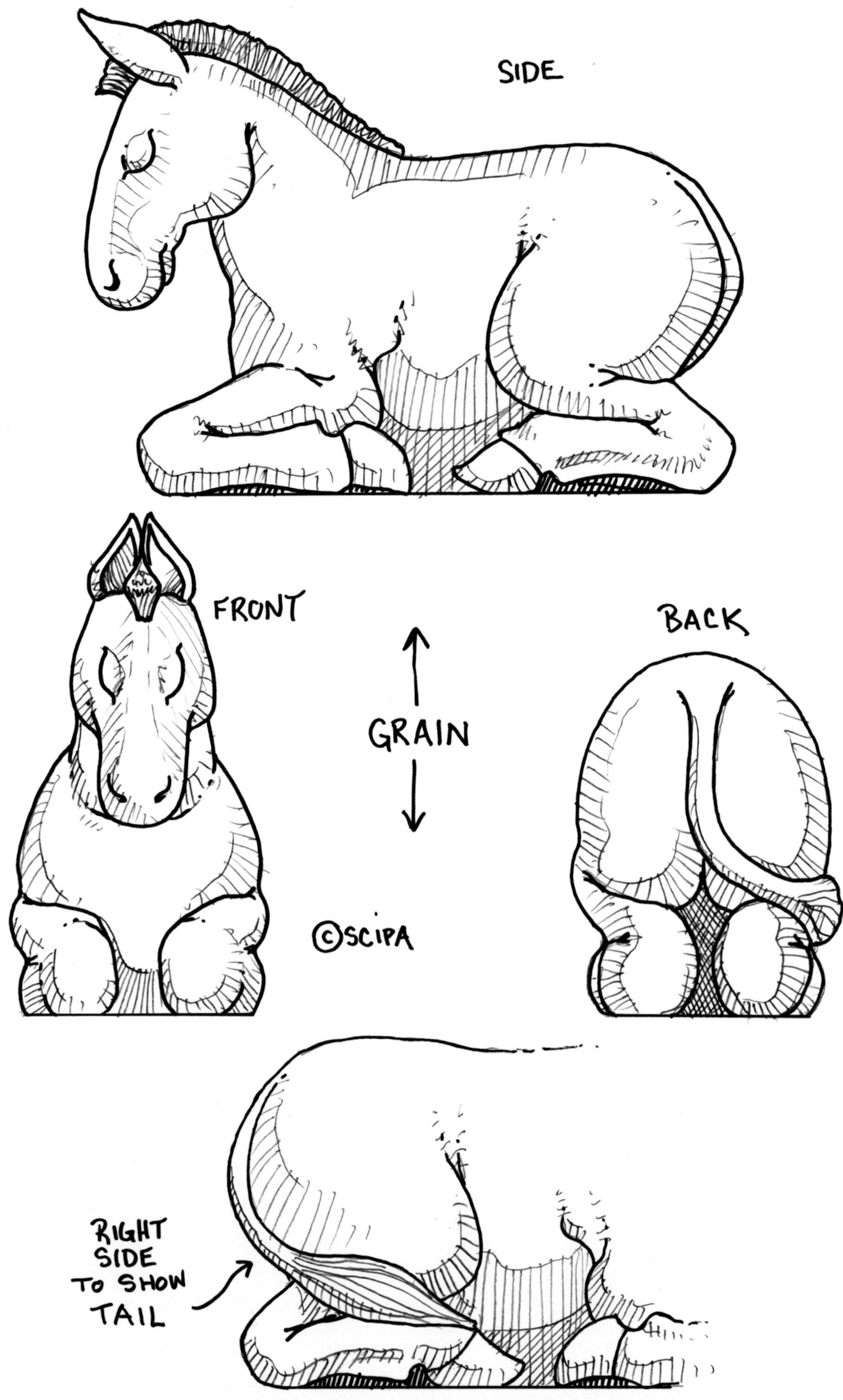
SIDE
FRONT
BACK
GRAIN
©SCIPA
RIGHT SIDE TO SHOW TAIL

DONKEY

Pattern on Page 78

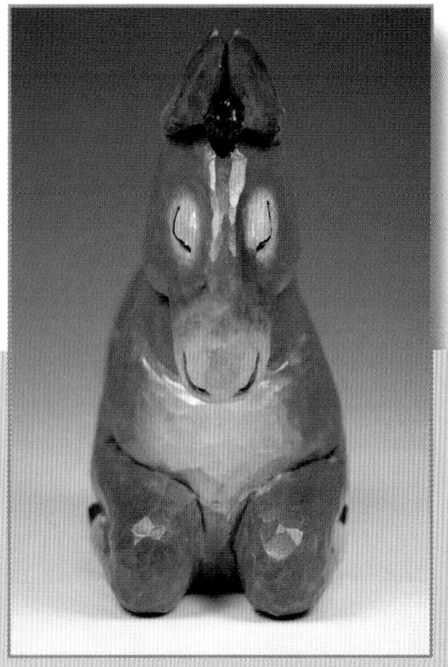

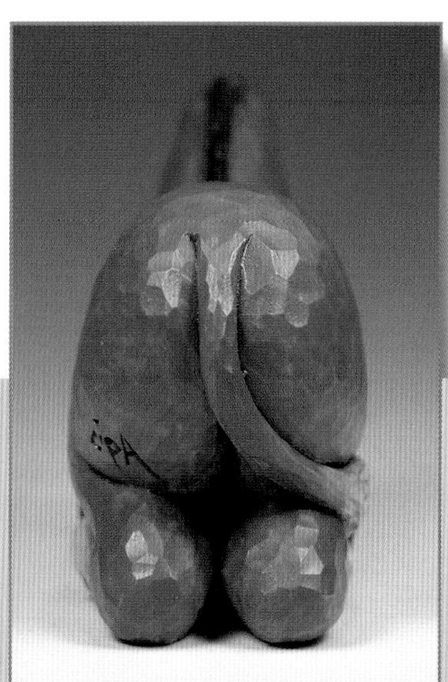

This design is similar to the ox, because their legs in the seated position closely resemble each other. Once you have mastered the ox, this one should come easily to you. The ears stand at attention and are carved together for strength. The block measures 5" x 2" x 3 $^{1}/_{2}$".